JILLY RISBEY

'Schizophrenia'... Exploding the Myth

A catalogue record of this book is available from the British Library

First Edition: February 2006

Second printing: September 2006

ISBN: 1-84375-195-X

To order additional copies of this book please visit:
http://www.upso.co.uk/nancymellor

Published by: UPSO Ltd
5 Stirling Road, Castleham Business Park,
St Leonards-on-Sea, East Sussex TN38 9NW United Kingdom
Tel: 01424 853349 Fax: 0870 191 3991
Email: info@upso.co.uk Web: http://www.upso.co.uk

'Schizophrenia'...
Exploding the Myth

by

Nancy Mellor

UPSO

I dedicate this book to Richard
who has suffered extreme trauma at the hands of
his abusers and the psychiatric system.

It's frozen
Your face
You
The true you
I can't reach you
The ice is too strong
You built the ice to protect yourself
It's too tough
Cold to the touch
Dare to be
Sensitive to the touch
Melt your heart
Strong is not hard

Book Launch Speech

Thursday 21st September, 2006 at Waterstones, Leeds

Ladies and Gentlemen, welcome to the book launch of 'Schizophrenia - Exploding the Myth'. For the next ten or fifteen minutes I would like to explain to you why I wrote this controversial book.

Firstly, I would like you to try and imagine that every day or night you are subject to unspeakable, horrific, sexual, physical and emotional abuse. You can't tell your family because the abuser has threatened that their lives will be in danger if you do. The abuser might even be a member of your family or a relative, or maybe he/she is a respected citizen, for example someone who is a teacher, a member of the clergy or someone who does a lot of charity work. You can't tell because you have been brought up to respect adults and to believe they are right. The abuse might take the form of being raped by several men in the back of a van, being hit over the head with heavy objects, being operated on with a drill, being hung upside-down from a light fitting, having instruments inserted in your anus, being buried in a coffin for a whole hour, being forced to take part in rituals, having your head pushed down a toilet, being forcibly drugged, choked, electrocuted, suffocated, nearly drowned, burned, completely undermined and ridiculed.

Maybe the abuse doesn't happen every single day. Maybe you never know when it is going to happen. You lay awake in bed at night on tenterhooks, your heart palpitating so much you think you're going to have a heart attack; waiting, listening for the sound of their footsteps, the turn of a key, the click of a door handle. You might try to distract yourself by watching television, studying, having fun with your family and friends. You let your guard down for a few minutes or an hour or two. But then you get that terrible sinking feeling, that ache in the pit of your stomach when you remember what agony might be in store for you later. Isn't it better to stay constantly aroused, expecting the next trauma, hypervigilant, never letting your guard down so it is not so unbearable and heart wrenching when next it happens?

Maybe you stop showing any emotion to the abusers so they can't have the power of knowing they've hurt you. Maybe you enjoy some of the sexual part and feel terribly guilty and dirty for this. You may even start to doubt your identity. Maybe they hurt your body so much that your mind goes away somewhere and you retreat into a fantasy world. Your mind and soul might even leave your body and you might be able to see the abuser doing things to your body. But you are removed - maybe on the ceiling or in a corner of the room. You might re-live the abuse after the event and hear the voices of the abusers insulting and ridiculing you. These flashbacks of the abuse might be so vivid that you feel and act like it is happening all over again. You might even shout out loud for them to stop and cry out in excruciating pain when there is nobody there. You may withdraw from the world, hiding in your room with the curtains drawn, not daring to go outside. You could end up living the abuse twenty-four hours a day and doubting your own sanity.

All of this change in behaviour and personality will not go unnoticed by those closest to you. They will know nothing of the abuse and so will suggest that you go to see your GP or you may go under your own steam. Because you are nervy and frightened, the doctor decides to make an appointment for you to see a psychiatrist. So you enter the psychiatrist's office. You are extremely nervous as you are going to disclose the abuse for the very first time. You describe the rape and the physical and mental torture you've suffered. It is possible that you go into detail, mentioning being buried in a coffin or being operated on with a drill. You might even have a flashback while you are there and flit from one topic to another without being able to concentrate.

As this sounds extremely far-fetched and no-one else is able to confirm it, the psychiatrist writes down HALLUCINATIONS, PARANOIA, DISORDERED SPEECH on his note pad. You describe these horrific events with a sense of detachment, showing no emotion. He writes down FLATTENING OF AFFECT. You describe how you rise up out of your body during the abuse so you can't feel anything. He writes down CATATONIA. Then you conclude by saying that you hear voices criticising you, saying you deserve it all because you're a bad person. He writes down HEARING VOICES.

The psychiatrist scans his notes and says, "Well, it's a textbook case of schizophrenia. You exhibit six of the classic symptoms. There is no cure I'm afraid but I'm going to prescribe you a neuroleptic drug. It should stop the hallucinations and help you to sleep better. I think it would be best if you went into a hospital for three months initially so we can monitor your behaviour more closely."

You leave the psychiatrist's office feeling confused, mistrusted and violated. It took a huge amount of courage for you to divulge the abuse to someone and you weren't listened to or believed. Maybe you had been hallucinating and you are ill. After all, you no longer know what reality is. You only know one thing for certain - you will never tell the truth about yourself to a psychiatrist again!

So now you're in hospital. At least you're away from the abuse, or so you think!! You see a couple of the in-patients acting strangely, screaming and tearing their hair out, being chased by the nurses who pin them down and inject them. Then they are physically strait-jacketed. Some patients have a glazed, dull, lifeless expression and are half asleep. Some have twitches and make constant jerky movements (MOTOR ABNORMALITIES). This is called Tardive Dyskinesia and is an irreversible side effect of neuroleptic medication. Some sleep for eighteen to twenty hours a day. Some cannot watch television because they see strange things on the screen. Some cannot pass water properly. Some are constantly trembling, drooling and shuffling from foot to foot. All of these are also side effects of neuroleptic medication. Psychiatrists occasionally walk by but they often ignore you or they might stop to ask you if you took your pill this morning. In fact, none of the staff talk to you for any length of time. Apparently, talking therapy doesn't help schizophrenics! If you cry, the psychiatrist thinks you are a danger to yourself or even suicidal; if you're angry, he thinks you are aggressive and a danger to others and if you're laughing too happily, you are manic and need to be sedated.

Ladies and Gentlemen, the reason why I have written 'Schizophrenia - Exploding the Myth' is because some of the above happened to a close relative of mine, Richard. When I began to research into other cases of schizophrenia it became evident that Richard's was no isolated case. It seems that sexual abuse is extremely common - one in four females and one in six males have been sexually abused before the age of eighteen and some of this abuse is prolonged, horrific, sadistic and unspeakable torture which is often hard to comprehend and believe. Through my research, I discovered that most cases of schizophrenia are caused by abuse or trauma. In fact, the latest research by Paul Hammersly from the University of Manchester and New Zealand clinical psychologist, Dr. John Read, presented on 14th June of this year shows that two thirds of people diagnosed with schizophrenia have suffered physical or sexual abuse. However, it does not necessarily follow that if abuse was not disclosed, it did not exist. Because abuse can be so traumatic to the individual, it may have been wiped from all consciousness. In other words, the individual may not remember being abused. Some say that schizophrenia is a genetic illness. No schizophrenic gene has ever been discovered. The most recent genetic research cannot conclude that genes play a major role in schizophrenia - only that genetic endowment may make one more vulnerable to schizophrenia.

I would like to recommend that the whole mental health system is revamped. It is only natural that a human being who is subject to horrific abuse will develop symptoms such as paranoia, flattening of affect, hearing voices and hypervigilance. These are life and self preservation strategies. It was Shakespeare who said there is method in madness. Assigning the diagnostic label of schizophrenia serves no useful purpose. Firstly, all the symptoms of schizophrenia can be found in other diagnoses so it is not a reliable diagnosis and, secondly, any two people who have received the diagnosis of schizophrenia may have no symptoms in common so neither is it a valid diagnosis. Every human being is unique. They cannot possibly fit into categories or diagnoses. Professor Robin Murray, the Head of General Psychiatry, London stated that the schizophrenia label is unhelpful as it can act as a barrier to receiving the correct treatment at the correct time. He also said that if he was diagnosed with schizophrenia, he would ask for another doctor. So why are psychiatrists in England still assigning this label if this is his opinion? Once someone has received a diagnosis of schizophrenia, they are strongly discriminated against. They cannot obtain mortgages or insurance and frequently cannot find work. They also believe they have an incurable disease from which they can never recover and so lose all hope and motivation.

I suggest that, like Japan has recently done, the diagnosis of schizophrenia is scrapped. Rather than having a diagnostic manual for mental illness, it would be far more effective to formulate a manual which lists symptoms individually and explains the possible causes and the best treatments for these. I would like to see all mental hospitals abolished. Phil Thomas, a consultant psychiatrist, found that doctors prescribe more medication when there are fewer staff on duty in hospitals and defined a high dosage of medication as social control. A recent letter to a magazine problem page headed, "Devastating Diagnosis" described a situation where someone's son had been diagnosed with schizophrenia. The advice was, and I quote, "Find out if there is an early intervention team near where you live. These teams specialise in helping people with schizophrenia. They focus on keeping the person out of the long-term mental health system so that they can recover and fulfil their potential." If it is a widely known fact that the mental health system has a detrimental effect on a person's chance of recovery, why is it still in existence? Last year the Healthcare Commission revealed significant gaps in the provision for mental health in England.

So what would we replace psychiatry and mental hospitals with? From my research, there are three principal methods which stand out as the most effective for treating people who have been abused. None of these are available on the NHS and it is impossible to attain funding to access these therapies privately. The three methods are Hearing Voices Groups, Confrontation Therapy and Psychoanalytic Psychotherapy. These are described in detail in my book but I will attempt to summarise them briefly now.

Firstly, the Hearing Voices Network organises group and individual work. There are now one-hundred-and-fifty-six groups around the country. At group meetings, people can discuss their experiences with others. They initially must acknowledge the presence of their voices, then explore their origin, find meaning in them, understand them and then hopefully eliminate any negative voices. If some persist, the person is taught how to cope with them. Any strange behaviour by the person is acknowledged, validated, normalised, understood and de-stigmatised by the others. Rufus May, a psychologist, said, "I think that when people get together and share ideas, they can achieve amazing things. I've learnt more from the Hearing Voices Network than I have in my six years of psychology training." Another participant described her first meeting as making more sense than a lifetime of sessions with psychiatrists.

Secondly, Confrontation Therapy (which is only available in America at present) is designed to intrude on a person's sick behaviour, disrupt any psychosis and produce different sets of behaviour that are more consistent with the expectations and demands of society. People who have been in hospital for a long time may not talk or may constantly exhibit dysfunctional behaviour. Their survival system is so strong that, when help is offered, they may fight against it or they may not even recognise that it is there as they are so preoccupied with protecting themselves. The confrontation therapist demonstrates that he is stronger than this survival system and breaks down the defences that have been built. This causes the person to feel safe enough to trust again and form a relationship with the therapist. One victim of abuse stated that she wanted a doctor to force his way in because she did not feel she had the strength. She said, "A doctor must be a rock that never rolls away no matter how much he is pushed. He should fight his way into what she felt, not ask permission or deliberate as this would cause her to feel guilty."

Thirdly, Psychoanalytic Psychotherapy is, in my opinion, the final part of the treatment process although I am sure it could work alongside help from the Hearing Voices Network. Victims of abuse are constantly attempting to solve their problems but they deal with symbols because confronting the real problems is too frightening. Psychoanalytic psychotherapy is invaluable in interpreting these symbols. Interpretations can synthesise the split in the self. Only when the symbolic act, or symptom, and the original traumatic experience are re-connected in consciousness can the person begin to recover. Understanding origins can sometimes lead to cures. Joan, a patient of Laing's, said, "Meeting you made me feel like a traveller who's been lost in a land where no-one speaks his language. Worst of all, the traveller doesn't even know where he should be going. He feels completely lost and helpless and alone. Then, suddenly, he meets a stranger who can speak English. Even if the stranger doesn't know the way to go, it feels so much better to be able to share the problem with someone; to have him understand how badly you feel. If you're not alone, you don't feel hopeless anymore. Somehow it gives you life and a willingness to fight again."

I would like these three methods of treatment to form the backbone of the training courses for psychiatrists, psychologists and nurses in the future. Patients must be given hope and responsibility again. Psychiatrists, psychologists and nurses must relax their prior beliefs about mental illness and act with intuition and spontaneity, tailoring treatments to each individual patient.

There is still an awful lot we don't know. At the end of my book I have recommended valuable research that might be undertaken in the future to discover further strategies that will work for these people but, for now, we must be content with abolishing what we know doesn't work. I would like to conclude with a quote by a local man, J.B. Priestley, who said, "Both the fanatical believers and the fixed-attitude people are loud in their scorn of what they call 'woolly minds'. Being woolly has no hard edges. It is easy, pliant, yet it has its has its own toughness. Because it bends, it does not break. The woolly mind realises that we live in an unimaginable, gigantic, complicated, mysterious universe. To try to stuff the vast bewildering creation into a few neat pigeon holes is absurd. We don't know enough and to pretend we do is mere intellectual conceit. The best we can do is keep looking out for clues for anything that will light us a step or two in the dark."

Thankyou for listening, Ladies and Gentlemen.

Contents

Author's Story

My intention in writing this book was to discover why 'schizophrenic' symptoms, especially hallucinations, develop and how they can be most effectively treated. This logically split into three principal questions which I have attempted to answer:

"How valid is the diagnostic category of 'schizophrenia'?"
"What causes 'schizophrenia'?"
"What is the most effective treatment for 'schizophrenia'?"

To the layman, some sections of this book may be quite a challenge to read, namely Chapter 2: 'Possible causes of Schizophenia' and Chapter 5: 'Psychoanalysis with Schizophrenics'. I would implore you to persevere with the book, even if you feel the need to skip to the more practical sections. I explored all possible causes and theories of 'schizophrenia' in order to assess which were the most genuine.

Over a hundred years of multidisciplinary research into the aetiology of 'schizophrenia' has yielded a small amount of conclusive evidence. A high proportion of the literature on 'schizophrenia' is biological in nature, both empirical investigations and treatment (medication). There is little written on psychoanalytic theories of 'schizophrenia' and an even smaller amount on therapeutic treatments. Therefore my research consisted of exploring many, sometimes diverse, topic areas to obtain detailed answers to my questions. I examined conditions such as 'PTSD', 'sexual abuse' and 'hearing voices' whose symptoms are almost identical to the symptoms of 'schizophrenia', to compare different approaches to diagnosis and treatment. The book is thus multi-dimensional but I believe all the dimensions to be of relevance in demonstrating how the present biological approach to 'schizophrenia' is ill-equipped to effect improvement in its sufferers.

A vast number of the empirical investigations are flawed. Even when their sampling and statistical techniques are scientifically robust, the interpretation of the data is questionable. No meaningful research can be conducted comparing 'schizophrenics' to others without first establishing the reliability and validity of the diagnosis. Also, patients cannot be regarded as physical material. Difficult diagnostic issues and patient heterogeneity limit the interpretation of data from any study of 'schizophrenic' patients.

The narrow clinical approach is especially alarming considering how little is known about 'schizophrenia'. It appears that some symptoms of 'schizophrenia' derive from taking neuroleptic medication, being institutionalised, alienated, stigmatised and labelled rather than listened to. Psychiatrists rarely investigate the origins of hallucinations but spend their time deliberating over which diagnoses most adequately describe their patients.

Tracy May states, "I remember the psychiatrist taking notes and not once did he really look at me...Never was I asked to change my behaviour, nor was it challenged...I believe that maybe if I had been confronted directly by a therapist, I would not have spent a good part of my life being sick. Although it is tragic that I lost a lot of years, what is really tragic is that people working with schizophrenics are not reaching their patients" (May, 2002).

When Richard, a close family member of mine, first saw a psychiatrist, he spoke of being followed, harassed, victimised and abused. These statements were perceived as paranoid delusions (ie. he was not believed) and instead of the psychiatrist delving into the reasons why Richard was saying this, he immediately made the diagnosis of 'schizophrenia'. It did not occur to the psychiatrist that Richard's affirmations were indeed fact and that he was actually being subject to horrific sexual, emotional and physical abuse at the hands of one of his so-called 'friends' (for example: being raped and beaten repeatedly, being forced to take part in rituals, being threatened that his family's lives would be in jeopardy if he disclosed these events).

Once someone has received a diagnosis of 'schizophrenia', they are strongly discriminated against (they cannot obtain mortgages, insurance and frequently cannot find work) and are often locked away in a mental institution. They can be forced to take neuroleptic medication which can cause irreversible side-effects such as the condition, 'Tardive Dyskinesia', where the patient constantly makes involuntary movements. This medication can also reduce hallucinations and induce a sense of apathy and docility, sometimes making the patient sleep for up to twenty hours a day. Those who experience hallucinations have more likely than not suffered traumas such as sexual abuse and need to put their feelings into words rather than having their memories suppressed. In essence, taking medication can encourage sufferers to avoid their problems rather than face them.

Trauma can cause someone to experience dissociation. (1) Once someone has divorced their self from their body, they may begin to hallucinate. In order for a person to come to terms with the abuse they have suffered, they must describe their experience in words. It is a critical feature of the healing process.

Eleven years ago Richard started seeing a psychotherapist (six years after his breakdown) and, after eleven months, he remembered being raped. The floodgates opened and he has been recalling horrific events ever since. He still experiences intense flashbacks where he is re-exposed to the abuse he suffered. Consequently, to outsiders, his behaviour can appear rather odd. Someone who has been given a diagnosis of 'schizophrenia', like Richard, cannot receive appropriate treatment on the NHS. The only options open to him are medication, cognitive behavioural therapy and having a social worker visit regularly. Sadly, the latter frequently feels intimidated by Richard because of his behaviour. Therapies such as psychodrama would allow Richard to understand his emotions and communicate them in a socially appropriate way. When a traumatised victim can be made aware of the meaning of his symptoms, the unexpressed emotions are released and no longer need to express themselves as symptoms. Richard also badly needs his confidence rebuilding as he was terrorised into not doing anything by his abusers.

The Hearing Voices Network has helped thousands of people to understand, accept, control and sometimes eliminate the voices (auditory hallucinations) they hear in order that they may live more normal lives. Richard now sees a young man who is a member of this Network. His understanding and empathy inspired Richard to open up to him immediately and, consequently, he has improved in many areas.

My book cannot give conclusive answers to questions because of the diversity of human experience. There are also limitations due to its theoretical nature. I hope I have highlighted the ineffective treatments and suggested more efficacious alternatives. I have realised there is an urgent need for more diverse and radical therapeutic treatments to be developed. A search for answers seemed to uncover more questions and consequently, in the 'Concluding Remarks', I have recommended valuable research that might be undertaken in the future by professionals in the field.

Synopsis

At present there are about three-hundred thousand sufferers of 'schizophrenia' in the UK (about 1% of the population). Although the DSM (2) explicitly defines the symptoms of 'schizophrenia', the disorder continues to provoke considerable philosophical and scientific controversy. No factor can be said to be a necessary and sufficient or even necessary but insufficient cause of 'schizophrenia'.

As this book questions the validity of the disorder, the term 'schizophrenia' has been placed in inverted commas throughout, suggesting that it is merely a collection of symptoms that have been artificially and erroneously grouped.

Chapter 1 gives a brief insight into how labelling a person with a diagnosis can remove all responsibility from that person, thus inhibiting their recovery process. Also, it is startling to discover the cost of 'schizophrenia' in terms of aetiological research and the lack of productivity of its sufferers.

Chapter 2 contains a summary of the aetiological and therapeutic studies of 'schizophrenia'. The most widely used treatment for 'schizophrenia' is neuroleptic medication even though its principal benefit diminishes only one symptom (hallucinations). Proponents of individual psychotherapy largely reject medications on the basis that they cover up the problems of 'schizophrenia'. Professional views have become polarised and debate between competing factions acrimonious.

No single cause has been established for 'schizophrenia'. Most variables known to affect human conduct have been implicated - genetic endowment, brain biochemistry, neural organisation, viral agents, birth complications, season of birth, life stresses, early childhood experiences, family structure and the reactions of others to deviant behaviour are many of the considered possibilities. Researchers have not been able to identify a 'schizophrenic' gene although there have been several false dawns. It is suggested that while particular genes might make one more vulnerable to the symptoms described in the diagnosis, there is no inevitability.

Chapter 3 examines the long-term harm of receiving a diagnosis of 'schizophrenia', including the administration of medication, institutionalisation and psychiatry. There is growing opposition to the way pharmaceutical companies set the agenda for the biologisation of mental health care. Drug culture is the prevailing ethos in the treatment of the mentally ill. Due to the serious (3) and irreversible side-effects of prolonged use of neuroleptics, there is an urgent need to evaluate psychological treatments for hallucinations, delusions, thought disorder and other psychotic symptoms. Medication can hinder the process of recovery and is often used as a short-term crisis management strategy.

Psychiatric services can be biased in favour of custody and control instead of care and cure. "Involuntary psychiatric therapy is not treatment but torture" (Szasz, 1962). Patients become weaker and more feeble because of psychiatrists' lack of expectations. A profession that heavily focuses on the limitations of the 'schizophrenic' cannot be proactively seeking information to develop a deeper understanding of the disorder. "Psychiatry is essentially a medical matter transacted through the technologies of medicine" (Bhugra and Bahl, 1999) and is ill-equipped to delve into the depths of 'schizophrenia'.

'Disorders' are merely statistical associations between symptoms yet the DSM is treated as the bible of mental illness. Patients' statements are often considered useful only as a basis for making and confirming a diagnosis. Symptoms are treated instead of causes. This is dehumanising because it reduces the mind to the role of by-product of the brain.

It is striking that information from the perspective of patients is largely absent in psychiatric literature. However, the internet is slowly building up websites dedicated to patients' stories of recovery and the abuse they suffered at the hands of professionals.

Chapter 4 searches for alternative explanations of 'schizophrenia'. There is a substantial overlap between the symptoms of 'schizophrenia', PTSD (Post Traumatic Stress Disorder) and the consequences of childhood abuse. There is significantly less stigma attached to such conditions. "Illnesses with an identifiable precipitant have a better prognosis than those due to constitutional factors in the individual" (Vaillant 1964, Van Os et al., 1994). Psychotic people are not merely disturbed but disturbed about particular aspects of their lives.

Followers of Laing and Szasz oppose recognition of the existence of the illness, 'schizophrenia', and its allied states. They also oppose specific treatments such as drug therapy and admission into hospital. Laing argued that a psychotic experiences a division between body and mind. 'Schizophrenia' actually means 'a split between the elements of thought and feeling' or 'confusion between inner and outer worlds' (Frude, 1998). No treatment for directly targeting ongoing dissociative symptoms has been elaborated or evaluated.

The value of psychotherapy for 'schizophrenics' has long been the subject of contentious debate within psychiatry. Most clinicians in the early twentieth century considered the disorder untreatable. Kraepelinian 'organic' psychiatrists viewed 'schizophrenia' as a progressive brain deterioration. Freudian psychoanalysts viewed it as a 'narcissistic neurosis' where transference (4), and hence cure, was impossible. Despite widespread therapeutic nihilism, a few early renegades were drawn to talk and spend time with the 'incurable'. Chapter 5 delves into Psychoanalysis and 'Schizophrenia'. Some psychoanalysts believe that 'schizophrenia' is an extreme psychological reaction to emotional stress. Psychoanalytic theory has generated intriguing and speculative analyses of case histories but little research. However, there are many cases (eg. Milner 1969, Rosenfeld 1952) where psychoanalytic techniques, when applied successfully, have gradually unravelled some 'schizophrenic' symptoms.

Chapter 6 examines a 'way-out' for people diagnosed with 'schizophrenia' by assessing several individual therapy programmes that have recently been established, including the Direct Confrontation Method and the Hearing Voices Network. Illness heterogeneity indicates that one type of treatment is not suitable for all patients and that treatment strategies and goals must be individualised. Clients who feel at ease and respected by their therapist are more likely to disclose information about sensitive issues.

The myths of the lack of meaning of 'schizophrenic' symptoms and the incurability of the disorder are still rife. "If one does not understand a person, one tends to regard him as a fool" (Jung, cited in Chadwick, 1997). If one does not look for something, one cannot find it.

Chapter 1

Background

'Schizophrenia' - the Label

Terms such as 'schizophrenia' and 'hysteria' have been socially constructed yet, through regular communication, one believes that these stigmatising labels exist as separate and scientifically valid disorders. "The tendency has always been strong to believe that whatever received a name must be an entity or being, having independent existence of its own. And if no entity answering to the name could be found, men did not for that reason suppose that none existed, but imagined that it was something peculiarly abstruse and mysterious" (Mill).

Janet Frame knew she was not a 'schizophrenic'. "Against this opinion, however, I now had the weight of the 'experts' and the 'world' and I was in no state to assert myself" (Frame, 1982). Sarah, a woman in her mid-twenties, who had suffered a 'schizophrenic' breakdown said, "You wake up every morning and you think, 'Oh God, I'm a 'schizophrenic'!' If the doctor hadn't told me, I would just have woken up and thought, 'Well, I'm just going through some sort of illness and I'll probably get over it.' But once you get diagnosed, you start thinking all-sorts from different corners about the illness and it just gets worse and worse" (cited in Bentall, 1990). One needs to re-establish oneself as an ordinary agent whose life is not wholly defined by one's clinical condition.

Unfortunately, society does not help those who have negative extraordinary experiences. Ignorance in society and, more importantly, in professionals, leads to stigmatisation. Sadly, 'schizophrenics' are strongly discriminated against. They cannot obtain insurance or buy a house. Currently there is little anti-discrimination legislation for people with mental health problems.

There is a strong case for severing connections with other mentally ill people if one is to lose the 'schizophrenic' label. If one associates with other ex-patients, one might risk incorporation into a mental-patient sub-culture and into marginalised self-definitions. This reduces the possibility of recovery. Those who have suffered themselves and are on the road to recovery are often most valuable in inspiring improvement in others. However, these people remain quiet about their own past because of the stigma. "Stigma is the great disease that is destroying any chance of recovery, forcing those who have mental health problems to hide their problems" (Coleman, 1999). Hiding a significant part of one's history may engender an internal sense of dissonance and create formidable problems of self-disclosure for people whose capacity for forming relationships is already precarious.

Frude (1998) states, "There is no cure for schizophrenia." Manfred Bleuler, the son of Eugen, concluded that 25% of sufferers recover permanently, 65% consistently alternate between recovery and psychotic lapses and 10% remain severely psychotic. "Anyone who agrees to work with the chronic schizophrenic agrees to take on a supposedly hopeless case. This is what you are taught, what the research says" (Slater, 1996). Tracey May, a recovered 'schizophrenic', said, "As a survivor, it is very upsetting to know that people are not getting the help they so desperately need...I tried to speak of my recovery process but was turned down flatly...Some (internet) sites even have warnings that people who claim they have recovered should not be believed because it gives sufferers false hope" (May, 2002). There is no contemplation of a cure in psychiatric studies. In fact, a recovery from 'schizophrenia' is so rare that psychiatrists routinely question the validity of the original diagnosis. Thus misdiagnosis is more generally accepted than recovery. Once a person has received the diagnosis, he/she will be able to do little to change it. (5) The method of diagnosing 'schizophrenia' is investigated in Chapter 3.

Perceiving oneself as a genetic 'schizophrenic' is hardly conducive to recovery in the long-term. "Mental illness is not something a person has, but is something he does" (Szasz, 1962) or something that has been done to him. "Only when we call minds 'sick' do we systematically mistake metaphor for fact; and send for the doctor to 'cure' the 'illness'. It's as if a television viewer were to send for a TV repairman because he disapproves of the programme he is watching...The question 'What is mental illness?' is shown to be inextricably tied to the question 'What do psychiatrists do?'" (Szasz, 1962). In China and other communities, mental illness is a taboo expression. Japan has recently scrubbed the diagnosis of 'schizophrenia'.

Cost and Research

"The cost of schizophrenia has been estimated at $11.6 to $19.5 billion annually. About two-thirds of this cost is due to lack of productivity by schizophrenic patients and about one-fifth to treatment costs" (Mosher and Gunderson, cited in Szasz, 1979).

In 1999, the total cost of schizophrenia to the UK NHS was £2.7 billion with around a third of this providing services for 'schizophrenic' disorders and 5% being used for anti-psychotic medication (Association of the British Pharmaceutical Company, 1999). Anti-psychotic (neuroleptic) medication is developed and sold by pharmaceutical companies who gain an enormous income from 'pushing' medication.

For the past fifty years, researchers have been pursuing a ghost within the body of psychiatry. The wrong questions are being asked. The Dean of the Institute of Psychiatry recently made a claim for increased expenditure on biological research into the causes of 'schizophrenia' instead of using this funding to improve services (Bentall, 1990).

Recent textbooks on 'schizophrenia' (eg. Kerr and Snaith, 1986) seldom refer to psychosocial determinants of symptoms or outcome. The Medical Research Council recommended ten areas of potential future research: genetic investigations, neuropathological studies of post-mortem brains, studies of synaptic connections; in particular brain regions, brain imaging studies, clinical trials of preventative medication and other care, clinical studies of abnormalities of thought and intervention using EMG and MEG, neuropsychological studies of dopamine pathways, evaluations of services to patients, more epidemiological studies and studies of symptom identification (Bentall, 1990).

It seems that every possible cause of 'schizophrenia' has already been investigated. Continued research into the aetiology of 'schizophrenia' is likely to prove fruitless. Placing the blame on biology is debilitating to enquiry. There has been patchy development of complementary therapies. Developing the range and choice of therapies would be much more worthwhile. When questioning the cause of 'schizophrenia', researchers fail to use their most informative source - the patient. An interesting and valuable line of enquiry would be to investigate how people recover from 'schizophrenia' and why some do and others cannot.

Chapter 2

Review of Research on 'Schizophrenia'

Brief History

The concept of 'dementia praecox' (meaning 'premature dementia') was first outlined by Kraepelin in an edition of his famous textbook of psychiatry dated 1896. Kraepelin (1898) noticed that auditory hallucinations and peculiarities of speech were indicative of temporal lobe damage. Eugen Bleuler investigated 'dementia praecox' and concluded that it was not a single, homogeneous condition but made up of a number of related forms of illness. He later renamed it 'schizophrenia' (1911) to emphasise the disintegration of the personality resulting from the loosening of associations. He maintained that primary symptoms are organic in origin and the secondary symptoms reflect attempts to adapt to the primary symptoms. Alzheimer (1897), Kraepelin (1919) and many others were also convinced that 'schizophrenia' was an organic illness.

Some Positive Symptoms (6) Explained

Hallucinations

Hallucinations appear to relate to contextual cues and are thus greatly diverse in nature from person to person (Bourguignon 1970, Al-Issa 1978). There are numerous theories of why people suffer from auditory hallucinations or 'hearing voices'. Auditory hallucinations are often accompanied by small movements of the speech muscles. This is known as 'subvocalisation' (McGuigan, 1966). Thus some hypothesise that one hears his/her own sub-vocal speech or super-ego. Hoffman (1986) proposed that hallucinations are the result of a deficit in speech production and thought disorder and consequently sufferers hear their own thoughts as alien voices. However, Bentall and Slade (1986) suggested that there is not a correlation between thought disorder and hallucinations. This hypothesis also fails to account for visual hallucinations and hallucinations experienced by 'normal' subjects. Research does not support the fact that hallucinations are abnormal images (Slade 1976, Catts et al. 1980). Clinical evidence shows that hallucinations increase in frequency and vividness when a person is under stress (Reese 1971, Siegel 1984) and becomes physiologically aroused. More detailed theories of hallucinations are discussed in Chapters 4 and 6.

Delusions

Little empirical research has been conducted on delusions. Delusions may be secondary symptoms generated by conscious or unconscious attempts to make sense of complex or confusing situations.

Freud's views on paranoid delusions account for only some delusions. He described paranoid delusions (1911) when analysing Schreber's autobiography (1902/1955). He believed that they result from repressed homosexual impulses striving for expression. The anxiety stemming from their threatened expression is handled primarily by the defence mechanism of projection: attributing to others, feelings that are unacceptable to one's ego. Since to love someone of the same sex is unacceptable to the ego, the emotion is altered into hating the person but this is unsatisfactory so the emotion is transformed into hating the person because the person hates him/her first. The hate is thus justified. The person who is unconsciously a love object becomes a persecutor. However, in delusions of grandiosity (megalomania), the contradiction of the homosexual impulse is experienced and the person decides to love no-one. As this is impossible due to libido having to be invested in or attached to something or someone, the psychic reality becomes that he loves himself. It is usually helpful to let 'schizophrenic' patients know that they are lonely and that their loneliness is normal. They always feel understood when their therapist talks of loneliness (Karon, 2001). The most important source of delusions is transference (Freud, 1912): reliving feelings, fantasies and experiences from the past with no awareness that it is the past.

In the DSM-IV it states that delusions are erroneous beliefs due to the misinterpretation of experiences. However, psychiatrists are not the most competent judges of whether a person's beliefs are erroneous as they have little time to question their patients in detail. Delusions are perceived as bizarre if they are "clearly implausible, not understandable and do not derive from ordinary life experiences" (DSM-IV, 1994). If they are rated as bizarre, this is enough to satisfy a diagnosis of 'schizophrenia'. This helps to conceal extreme cases of abuse. Victims dare not reveal the horrific events they endured and even if they do summon the courage to tell a psychiatrist, they may be diagnosed with 'schizophrenia'!

Psychiatrists often believe bizarre tales to be irrational without enquiring into their origin. "Just because people are paranoid, it does not mean that they are not being persecuted" (Bentall, 1990). Delusions do not spring out of the minds of patients at random.

Disordered Speech

"The 'schizophrenic' quite typically has difficulty in thinking clearly, logically and cohesively. (7) He will also find it difficult or impossible to concentrate...and talk a stream of nonsense known only to himself" (Enoch, cited in Moate and Enoch,

1990). However, Rosenfeld (1952) managed to establish a deep understanding of his patient and demonstrated that his patient's speech was meaningful, as did Lacan (with Aimee in the 1930's) and Freud (to some extent, with Schreber's text (1911)).

Harrow and Prosen (1978) found that associations from the past are intermingled in disordered speech, pointing towards an impairment of perspective which prevents sufferers from deciding which speech is appropriate to the circumstances (cited in Bentall, 1990). Obviously, these associations are of prime importance in discovering the reason behind the psychosis and must not be suppressed by medication.

If one listens carefully to the patient, his speech always makes psychological sense in light of his life experiences. The psychotic symptoms are always a reasonable reaction to events of the patient's life. "In order to understand the patient's 'symptom' we must be acquainted with all the historically unique aspects of his personality development and social circumstances" (Szasz, 1962).

Shakespeare said there is method in madness. It is the analyst's task to unravel the game of life that the patient is playing. The analysis of the paranoiac delusion and hallucinatory productions reveals an order for the psychotic subject, a function of reconstructing a world that has collapsed (Freud, 1911). "If we look at the extraordinary behaviour of the psychotic from his own point of view, much of it will become understandable" (Laing, 1959).

Slater who worked with 'schizophrenics' said, "The schizophrenic speaks a mumbo-jumbo language psychologists call a 'word-salad', nouns and verbs, fragments from the past, snippets of dreams all tossed into the lush wet mess... In their tossed-up word-salads I sometimes catch glimpses of continuous themes, diced-up apples of desire, green leaves of love. I want to go there, tread through those gardens...The staff in this unit advise me to forget about doing 'deep work' - work that either focuses on the patients' own internal worlds or attempts to foster real relationships among them" (1996).

Joan, a patient of Laing's, said, "We schizophrenics say and do a lot of stuff that is unimportant, and then we mix important things in with all this to see if the doctor cares enough to see them and feel them" (cited in Laing, 1959). This implies that a 'schizophrenic' is capable of assessing whether or not their speech is coherent.

"A good deal of schizophrenia is simply nonsense, red-herring speech, prolonged filibustering to throw dangerous people off the scent, to create boredom and futility in others" (Laing, 1959). Jung said that the 'schizophrenic' ceases to be 'schizophrenic' when he meets someone by whom he feels understood. Then a lot of the bizarreness evaporates.

Thought Disorder

Harrow and Prosen (1979) showed that thought-disordered patients could provide rationales for their bizarre speech in terms of their past experiences (cited in Bentall, 1990). Berenbaum et al. (1985) investigated genetic factors involved in such symptoms and found no evidence for the inheritance of disordered discourse. (8) Von Domarus (1944) interpreted the thought disorder common in 'schizophrenics' as non-Aristotelian logic: for example, equating a stag with an Indian due to its swiftness of movement (cited in Szasz, 1962).

Disorganised thinking and loose associations are characteristic features of 'schizophrenia'. However, flashbacks might cause discontinuities in thought as one is intermittently exposed to the past (see Chapter 4). Even 'normal' people digress from one topic to another when talking due to their train of thought leading them in particular directions, often unbeknown to the listener. Therefore this symptom may be apparent in a 'normal' person who has not received a diagnosis.

Catatonia

Fromm-Reichmann (1950) reported that catatonic patients see and hear everything happening around them, even though they do not react. They feel as if they will die if they move. (9) Ratner, Karon, VandenBos and Denny (1981) investigated animals in a state of 'animal hypnosis'. When rabbits, lions, tigers, alligators, fish, octopuses and, in total, seventy species of birds are turned upside-down and pressed, they become rigid. They will not move, even if great pain is inflicted. After a period of time, the animals move in an unpredictable, rapid, violent motion which is reminiscent of the human catatonic excitement. Classical conditioning experiments show that they are conscious of external stimuli whilst rigid. Ratner explained that most animals are prey for some predator. Some predators will not attack something that does not move because they think it is already dead. Thus the catatonic stupor is a life and species preservation strategy that is built into just about all living animals, including human beings. Animal research has been criticised in relation to 'schizophrenia' due to language and thought disorder being principal symptoms. However, this study is unconcerned with these symptoms.

A catatonic man who constantly bowed admitted that he was balancing emotions of fear and loneliness. When upright, he felt lonely and so bowed to be close to others but when close to others he became fearful and so pulled away again to an upright position. When catatonic patients are 'out' they are totally at the mercy of anyone who wants to use them as an object of fun and derision. Someone who has created a defence such as this must learn to defend himself without having to resort to catatonia.

Karon interviewed a male catatonic patient who had been hospitalised for ten years. The patient began the therapy hour by yelling, "Why did you do it to me, dad?" Through assuming the transference reaction of the man's father, Karon asked, "What did I do?" The patient then disclosed that when he was eight, his father had returned home drunk one evening and had anally raped him. This patient stuttered whilst speaking words of Latin.

When asked if he had been an altar boy, he replied, "You swallow a snake and then you stutter. You mustn't let anyone know." He was extremely ashamed and guilty as he revealed he had performed fellatio on a priest. Karon interpreted orally: (10) "Anyone as hungry as you were would have done the same thing." At that point the stuttering ceased. It is hardly surprising that he was psychotic when his mother choked him for not eating, his father raped him and, when he turned to God, the priest was destructive. His records from the ten years of hospitalisation revealed no basis for his psychosis. This suggests that the real reason behind the patient's catatonia had not been investigated.

'Cultural relativism' describes the view that definitions of abnormality should vary according to different cultures: for example, the visions of a shaman could be perceived as hallucinations; sorcery and witchcraft may be delusional in one culture but not in another; hallucinations appear in the bible: stories of visions, seeing the Virgin Mary, hearing God speak, etc.

Negative Symptoms (11)

An example of a negative symptom is 'flattening of affect'.

Flattening of Affect

The symptoms of 'schizophrenia' may be understood as manifestations of chronic terror which can mask other feelings causing flattening of affect (see Chapter 4). This process is appropriate to the patient's inner experiences even if it is socially inappropriate. This contradicts the benefits of neuroleptic drugs which greatly diminish affect. The affect has already been dampened down by the patient him/herself.

Other negative symptoms: for example, 'social isolation' and 'hygiene neglect', are indicative of low self-esteem and depression. (12)

Possible Causes of 'Schizophrenia'

Family Studies (genetic)

If a close member of one's family is 'schizophrenic', the chance of developing 'schizophrenia' increases from 1% to 10% and if two close members have 'schizophrenia', the probability rises to over 25%. According to Gottesman (1991), the percentage risk of suffering from 'schizophrenia' if one has two 'schizophrenic' parents is 46%.

If one is an identical twin (monozygotic MZ) of a 'schizophrenic', the probability of developing the disorder is 48% (17% for dyzgotic DZ). This leaves a substantial discordance rate of 52% which points to powerful non-genetic factors.

Suddath, Christison, Torrey, Casanova and Weinberger (1990) found more brain abnormalities of unknown origin in 'schizophrenic' MZ twins compared to the non-'schizophrenic' twins. However, the data reveals that this difference would disappear if they were statistically corrected for medication dosage.

Consanguinity studies assume that a disorder occurring in relatives of an affected individual provides evidence for heredity. They ignore non-genetic factors such as parental behaviour and external stresses. About 90% of 'schizophrenics' do not have an afflicted parent and 81% have neither a 'schizophrenic' parent nor sibling (Robbins, 1992). This also indicates non-genetic factors.

In a study by Gottesman and Shields (1972), 42% of MZ and 9% of DZ twins developed 'schizophrenia' but if the patient had been hospitalised for more than two years, the concordance rate was 77%. However, for a hospitalisation of less than two years, the rate was 27%, suggesting that hospitalisation has a negative effect on a person's mental state.

Klebanhoff (1957) discovered that mothers of 'schizophrenics' have pathological attitudes. However, he found similar attitudes in mothers of hospitalised, brain-injured and retarded children and concluded that it is the stress of dealing with a disordered child that contributes to their pathology. It is not clear whether he knew these mothers before they gave birth to their children.

The Genain Quadruplets (cited in Frude, 1998) all developed 'schizophrenia' but at different ages and all with different forms of the disease. The two that suffered most acutely were less favoured by their parents. This indicates how environmental factors may have relevance. The study of families in which there is a high prevalence of 'schizophrenia' can be misleading as it often leads to an over-emphasis of genetic factors.

Some genetic studies (eg. Kety, Wender, Rosenthal, Welner and Schulsinger, 1974) suffer from fatal scientific flaws and misleading reporting. For example, biological relatives are reported to have higher rates of 'schizophrenia' than adoptive relatives. However, the data for biological relatives is inflated by half-siblings of 'schizophrenics' who have a higher rate of 'schizophrenia' than full siblings or than parents. No genetic model can account for such a finding. In a similar study (Rosenthal et al., 1968), only three cases out of seventy-six were classed as 'clear-cut schizophrenia' by Welner.

The most impressive genetic 'experiment' was most horrific and insane. For several years, all the 'schizophrenics' (hundreds of thousands) in Nazi Germany were sterilized yet, a generation later, the rate of 'schizophrenia' was not affected (eg. Haefner and an der Heiden, 1997).

Researchers at Middlesex hospital, London, claimed that they had located the genetic locus of 'schizophrenia' on chromosome 5 (Sherington et al., 1988). However, Kennedy et al. (1988) also provided strong evidence of the converse which was also confirmed by St. Clair et al. (1989). Evidently, in the Middlesex study, individuals suffering from depressive disorders, drug addiction, alcoholism and phobias were included as cases of 'schizophrenia'. No evidence of genetic linkage was found, regardless of how broadly or narrowly 'schizophrenia' was defined. The ideology of biological reductionism often leads researchers to make inflated claims for their techniques making it difficult for the observer to distinguish science from rhetoric.

It has been reported in Iceland, Scotland, Wales and now generally across the world, that Neuregulin 1 on chromosome 8 can make a person twice as likely to develop 'schizophrenia' as someone who does not possess this gene (Murray, 2005).

The fact that no study is more than 48% certain that 'schizophrenia' is characterised by a genetic predisposition indicates that environmental factors must play a role in determining whether someone who is vulnerable to 'schizophrenia' will actually develop the disorder.

Since the brain is a plastic organ, structurally responsive to the environment and hence to mental process, it is conceivable that organic changes are secondary to the experiences or ensuing mental disturbances. (13) There is scant evidence that they are related to genetic abnormality.

Biochemical

Some hypothesise that overactivity in the brain dopamine systems causes 'schizophrenia'. Davis et al. (1991) conducted post-mortem studies on 'schizophrenic' patients and discovered high dopamine concentrations in various subcortical regions of the brain and high densities of dopamine receptors in these areas. Waddington (1991) used brain scans to examine the brains of living 'schizophrenic' patients and found an excess of such cells, even though some had never been administered anti-psychotic drugs.

Certain stimulant drugs, such as amphetamines, can cause a normal person to experience hallucinations and paranoia due to their production of dopamine. Therefore such drugs can increase the severity of these symptoms in 'schizophrenics' (Haracz, 1982). Neuroleptic drugs block dopamine receptors and thus alleviate the positive symptoms (hallucinations and delusions). It takes several weeks of consistent drug administration for hallucinations to be reduced, even though the dopamine receptors are blocked within hours of the first dose. One explanation for this is that 'schizophrenics' may have excess dopamine in only some areas of their brain and low levels in others. Davis et al. (1991) hypothesised that an abnormally low level of dopamine activity in the pre-frontal regions may lead to excessive dopamine activity in the mesolimbic region. Conversely, dopamine abnormalities could be due to neuroleptic medication (Galtaz 1983, Mackay 1982).

A number of investigations consistently show that there is no evidence of increased dopamine turnover. Some believe that 'schizophrenia' occurs when there is an imbalance between different neurotransmitter systems. However, changes in mood, behaviour, perception, arousal and cognition influence a host of neurotransmitters and their interactions and so are fundamental to all psychological and psychiatric conditions.

Others have suggested that biochemical agents such as serotonin, acetylcholine, GABA, neuropeptides and prostaglandins are related to 'schizophrenia'. All of these could contribute to the balance of activity between several neurotransmitter systems.

Many methodological problems plague biochemical data and many confounds, unrelated to whether or not a subject is 'schizophrenic', can produce biochemical differences. One must maintain a cautious attitude with regard to this data. Furthermore, studies on biochemicals can only indicate that a particular substance and its physiological processes are associated with 'schizophrenia'. Dopamine activity might change after, rather than before, the onset of the disorder. "No consistent biochemical substance has been isolated from the brains of sufferers...Many of the findings of the early biochemical investigations turned out to be the result of unusual diet or medication" (Enoch, 1990).

Structural Abnormalities

Birchwood et al. (1988) suggested that the balance of activity between the hemispheres of the brain may be disturbed in some 'schizophrenic' patients. Some patients have a low level of activity in their dominant (usually left) hemisphere. Other studies have discovered dysfunction in the frontal lobe of the brain or abnormalities of functioning in the medial temporal lobe (which plays a crucial role in integrating information) (Roberts, 1991). However, temporal lobe abnormalities could be caused by aberrant genetic mechanisms, and asymmetries that occur in normal development might cause a more severe effect on the dominant hemisphere.

Mayer et al. (1985) discovered that flat affect was associated with right-hemisphere impairment, the extra-pyramidal side-effects of medication and hospitalisation. Therefore environmental variables and socio-economic conditions are highlighted as causes (Warner, 1985). Concentration-camp victims have exhibited similar attitudes and patterns of behaviour.

Some studies have found an enlargement in neural fibres (corpus callosum) in 'schizophrenic' patients. Conversely, other studies have noticed 'schizophrenic' patients with abnormally thin corpus callosum. One explanation for this is that a thickened corpus callosum is associated with the early onset of 'schizophrenia' and negative symptoms, whereas a thin corpus callosum is associated with late onset and positive symptoms. Coger and Serafetinides (1990) have provided empirical support for this.

There are four cavities or 'ventricles' filled with cerebrospinal fluid inside the brain. If there is atrophy of the tissue surrounding the ventricle, it will increase in size. Large ventricles are associated with 'schizophrenia' (Reveley, 1985) yet Pearlson et al. (1989) failed to find such an effect. Also, Jernigan, Zatz,

Moses and Berger (1982) found no evidence of cortical atrophy or enlarged ventricles in their samples of 'schizophrenics'. Trimble and Kingsley (1978) found normal ventricular sizes. Seidman (1984) reported that 20-30% of 'schizophrenics' suffer from gross organic impairment and have accounted for cerebral atrophy by diet, institutionalisation, neuroleptic drugs and convulsion therapies. Some researchers (Tatetsu, 1964) have discovered similar structural abnormalities in non-psychotic traumatised patients such as war victims. Reveley (1985) suggested that ventricle enlargement was a result of a permanent dosage of phenothiazines.

There are findings of cortical atrophy and frontal metabolic hypoactivity (Kirch and Weinberger 1986, Venables 1987) yet the differences between 'schizophrenics' and normal people in this area are not remarkable and only mildly significant when large groups are statistically compared. The finding is not unique to 'schizophrenia' and could actually be caused by long-term administration of neuroleptics. It seems that structural abnormalities somehow induce a vulnerability to 'schizophrenic' symptoms but they are neither necessary nor sufficient to induce such symptoms. Many brain loci have been implicated.

A more recent study shows that patients treated with both traditional and newer neuroleptics had marked brain changes as compared to drug-free patients and healthy volunteers. These brain abnormalities seemed to be medication-induced hypertrophy (Gur et al., 1998).

Normal people possess a filter to screen out irrelevant information. It has been suggested that 'schizophrenia' may result from the mal-functioning of this hypothetical filter (McGhie and Chapman, 1961).

These studies have not implicated a single abnormality consistently present in all patients. No characteristic is universal and it seems that only a quarter of 'schizophrenics' have any form of gross brain abnormality (Seidman 1983).

A twenty-nine year old man who suffered from accusatory and obscene auditory hallucinations, agitation and violence who threatened his family was hospitalised and administered chlorpromazine. A post-mortem examination showed that his brain was "normal. Cell, axon and myelin stains were unremarkable" (Stevens, 1982).

Seidman (1984) stated that "the frequency of abnormal neurological examinations using soft signs is consistently between 36% and 75%" (Jackson and Pilgrim, cited in Bentall, 1988). Considering this range, the term 'consistent' seems extremely far-fetched here. He eventually declared that 'schizophrenics' do not form a homogeneous group.

Perinatal Stress

McNeil and Kaij (1978) reported that obstetric complications seem to interact with a genetic influence towards 'schizophrenia'. In MZ discordant twin studies, the twin whose birth was marked by the most obstetrical complications was likely to be the one who developed 'schizophrenia'. If both twins were 'schizophrenic', the one who suffered most obstetrical complications suffered from more acute and severe symptoms. This research has been replicated and critiqued.

The Viral Hypothesis

Kings and Cooper (1989) proposed that an infant who has developed a viral infection in the perinatal period is more likely to be diagnosed with 'schizophrenia'. It appears that more 'schizophrenic' patients are born in the winter, perhaps making them more susceptible to viral infections at birth. However, post-mortem studies have not confirmed that 'schizophrenics' possess abnormal viral content in their brain tissue.

Faulty Learning

Behaviourists, Ullman and Krasner (1975), proposed that if

children are given no or little social reinforcement, they will focus on inappropriate and irrelevant environmental cues. This may manifest itself in bizarre behaviour making outsiders avoid or respond erratically to the child. Thus a psychotic state may be reached in adulthood due to the repetitive cycle of unfavourable responses to the child from outsiders.

Szasz (1962) likened mental illness to speaking a foreign language. It would be foolish and fruitless to look for the cause of a person's peculiar linguistic behaviour. We merely think in terms of learning and meaning. In other words, speaking French is the result of living amongst people who speak French.

Labelling Theory

Scheff (1966) suggested that 'schizophrenia' is a learned social role. Labelling theory is a radical departure from the traditional concept of 'schizophrenia' and is essentially unconcerned with aetiology. Scheff believes the crucial factor to be the act of assigning a diagnostic label. This label will influence the way a person behaves and the way he/she is treated. This is supported by a recovered 'schizophrenic': "A traumatic event precedes the onset of voice hearing in a large number of cases...However, the initial traumatic event is overshadowed by the terrible trauma of having an expert label us schizophrenic...The fact is that when the experts label us, the damage done far outweighs the damage done by the original trauma. Having been pronounced mad, we become mad" (de Valdo, Hearing Voices, 2001).

Meehl questioned labelling theory citing one patient who continuously kept his finger up his anus to prevent his thoughts from running out and another patient who attempted to tear out all his hair because it belonged to his father (Davison and Neale, 1974). However, this bizarreness is often a defence to preserve the self (see Chapter 4).

Schizophrenogenic mothers
This type of mother (defined by Fromm-Reichmann in 1948) is self-centred, cold, domineering and replete with contradictions and ambiguities. She causes confusion and incomprehensibility.

The Double-Bind Hypothesis
Parents sometimes give contradictory messages. They say one thing when they mean another, talk in a conflicting tone to the meaning of a statement or demand two incompatible behaviours. (14) This can be so perplexing and distressing for a child that it may precipitate a psychotic breakdown. However, Helmerson (1983) has not found experimental evidence for this.

Expressed Emotion (EE)
The emotional climate in a patient's home can often trigger a relapse. The dimensions of the EE Scale are: frequency of critical comments; hostility; marked emotional involvement; warmth and positive remarks. These are rated from an audio-taped interview with a patient's relative. A relative is considered to be 'high EE' if they give more than six critical comments and/or more than one hostile comment and/or show more than three signs of emotional involvement. Ehlert (1987) spoke of the difficulty of recruiting families to test this scale. "It was impossible to co-operate with local psychiatric hospitals or with psychiatrists in private practice. The reasons for refusal were lack of interest, mistrust in behaviour therapy, unwillingness to work with a psychologist, and fear of loss of patients" (Bentall, 1990).

In a seminal study, Brown et al. (1972) discovered that the level of emotion expressed by a key relative at the time of hospital admission provided the single best predictor of symptomatic relapse during the nine months after the patient's discharge from hospital. 58% of patients living with a 'high EE' relative relapsed within the nine months compared to 16% living with a 'low EE' relative.

If families are educated about the symptoms of 'schizophrenia', their causes and the most effective methods of dealing with them, and are introduced to 'low EE' families who have coped admirably with a similar situation, more favourable results will ensue (Leff et al., 1982). During the two years following such a programme, only 14% had suffered a relapse compared to 78% of a control-group who did not take part in this family intervention programme. Seemingly, being well informed fosters greater understanding and compassion.

Stressful Events

Stressful events can cause 'schizophrenia' in someone who is vulnerable (Brown and Birley 1968, Rabkin 1980, Tennant 1985). Particular forms of stress such as over-involvement, criticism and hostility can trigger 'schizophrenic' symptoms. However, this is generally not supported. "When visiting people diagnosed as 'schizophrenic' in their homes it is often difficult not to be shocked by the appalling conditions in which they are forced to live. In such circumstances I have often found myself thinking, 'How can any treatment, no matter how effective, hope to overcome this?'"(Bentall, 1990). This is rarely mentioned in psychiatric textbooks. Psychiatrists cannot determine whether a reaction to an event or set of circumstances is plausible unless they have experienced something similar. They seldom take the care and time to investigate whether the patient has suffered stressful life events (see PTSD, Chapter 4).

Cultural Differences

African-Caribbeans have higher admission rates to British psychiatric hospitals and are diagnosed with 'schizophrenia' three to six times more than the White population (Bhugra et al., 1997). The unemployment rate for African-Caribbeans at the time of this study was 82%. Other factors such as low self-esteem, financial pressure, material deprivation, oppression, institutionalised racism, chronic stress and a culture of cannabis use (but there is no indication that they use more than Whites) are possible contributing factors.

There are decreased social networks in small, dispersed ethnic minority populations. The lower the proportion of non-White ethnic minorities, the higher the incidence of 'schizophrenia' in those minorities. More racist harassment and stereotyping would take place in a predominantly White environment (Bhugra and Bahl, 1999).

Psychiatrists are prone to invoking racial stereotypes when making diagnoses. African-Caribbean patients are more likely to be admitted to hospital under Section 136 than White patients and are less likely to be admitted routinely through their GP (Turner et al., 1992). Language difficulties may also affect the diagnosis as less descriptive accounts will be given by the patients themselves. Harrison et al. (1988) expressed concern about the over-concentration of admissions for treatment. A reason for this over-diagnosis could relate to the "lack of understanding by the psychiatrists of the presenting symptoms within the cultural and religious context of the person concerned" (Fernando, cited in Bhugra and Bahl, 1999). Also, Whites living in Japan are more likely to be admitted to psychiatric hospitals than those living in Britain (Van Os, 2005).

Thomas (1997) stated that the high doses of medication administered to young African-Caribbean men has almost certainly contributed to the sudden deaths of a number of Black men over the last ten years. According to an enquiry (Special Hospital Service Authority), this high dosage was administered because White health professionals perceived young Black men as dangerous and violent. Geraghty (1985) stated that White people were almost twice as likely to receive psychotherapy as ethnic groups.

Recent evidence has highlighted that Vitamin D is vital for brain development in the foetus. Black skin produces sufficient Vitamin D when exposed to strong sunlight but insufficient amounts in cooler climates (John McGrath, Dept. of Psychiatry, University of Queensland, 2001).

If African-Caribbeans have a genetic susceptibility to developing 'schizophrenia', one would expect an increased incidence of 'schizophrenia' in the Caribbean. There is no evidence of this. Rates of 'schizophrenia' similar to those of the White population in the UK were reported in Jamaica (Hickling and Rodgers-Johnson, 1995).

The United Nations conducted a study through the World Health Organisation and discovered that people diagnosed with 'schizophrenia' in Third World countries have higher rates of recovery than those who live in First World nations (Bentall, Jackson and Pilgrim, 1988). Perhaps families in under-developed countries need each member to be productive. Therefore there may be greater tolerance of deviance.

Cannabis Use

Those who use cannabis in adolescence are three times more likely to develop 'schizophrenia' in later life than those who do not. Cannabis has an effect upon the dopamine system (Murray, 2005).

Urban Areas

There is evidence to show that those who have been raised in a city centre are two/three times more likely to develop 'schizophrenia' than those who have been raised in the suburbs (Van Os, 2005). Poverty and crime are obviously more prevalent in Urban areas.

General Theories

Even left/right confusions, poor co-ordination, having a highly arched palate, having narrow or wide set eyes and subtle malformations of the ears have been named as possible causes of 'schizophrenia' (DSM-IV, 1994)!

Review of Research

Almost all 'schizophrenics' whose behaviour is summarised in Journals are found in hospital. 63% of 115 empirical studies in the Journal of Nervous and Mental Disease, the Journal of

Abnormal Psychology and the American Journal of Psychiatry did not provide the length of hospitalisation of their subjects. The other 37% had been hospitalised for 7.1 years on average. Most of the control groups were not hospitalised. Controls must match in the extent of institutionalisation, educational level and achievement, sexual and marriage history, occupational success, past and present drug regimens, misery and loneliness. Otherwise researchers are in danger of spending time unproductively. In general, studies present few or no other psychological hypotheses to account for differences in their study group and control group apart from the one in question.

The traditional 'schizophrenia' researcher's strategy is comparing heterogeneous groups of 'normals' with equally heterogeneous samples of 'schizophrenics'. If the disorder of 'schizophrenia' is equivocal, how can true 'schizophrenics' participate in these studies in the first place (see Chapter 3)? "There is a pressing need to develop research strategies in psychopathology which do not depend on the validity of traditional psychiatric diagnoses" (Bentall, 1990).

Also, how can comparisons be made between heterogeneous groups of 'normals' and equally heterogeneous groups of 'schizophrenics' when those experiencing a mixture of 'schizophrenic' and non-'schizophrenic' symptoms are the norm? The tendency towards psychotic behaviour is distributed along a series of continua which connect madness with ordinary mental life (Claridge, 1987). Categorisation contradicts this view. All the data seems to require a dimensional or a multidimensional model (Claridge) rather than categorical model of mental disorder to incorporate all borderline and related states.

It is extremely difficult to securely construct unequivocal causative statements without experimental manipulation. Study results on 'schizophrenics' are generalised as though 'schizophrenia' was a single illness. Such pervasive attitudes have produced response biases that have contributed extreme variance to research results. The whole brain is much more than the sum of its biological parts. "To view the patient as physiologic apparatus, the clinician as psychologically inert and the interaction as unaffected by this mutual refraction threatens to artificially modify the data" (Nevins, cited in Schachter, 1993).

Therapy Studies

It is becoming increasingly clear that psychological methods are effective in the treatment of the psychoses. Karon (1989) conducted a computer search of all available studies and found that the effectiveness of psychoanalytic psychotherapy is supported by empirical data. Deikman and Whitaker (1979) instituted a regimen of almost purely psychological treatment in one 'experimental' ward of a psychiatric hospital (cited in Karon, 2001). Despite dire warnings that their failure to medicate constituted malpractice, their ward programme decreased re-hospitalisation. There were no suicides or suicide attempts. Another ward that was more fully staffed and used expert psychopharmacology had three suicides in the same period as well as sending its more disturbed patients to a long-term state hospital. Despite its success, this experiment was discontinued and never imitated. Surely this lack of acknowledgment constitutes severe malpractice and neglect!

Sometimes it is argued that research has proven that psychotherapy with 'schizophrenics' is unhelpful. These studies (eg. Grinspoon, Ewalt and Shader 1972, May 1968) often have many methodological flaws, the worst being that they involve so-called 'psychotherapists' and 'supervisors', none of whom have ever before treated a 'schizophrenic' patient by psychotherapy. Either they have little training in psychotherapy or little experience in treating a variety of patients with different kinds of therapy. It is also difficult to see how as short a period as two years of psychotherapy can undo a person's whole life experience.

The McLean study (Gunderson et al., 1984) seemed to

demonstrate that dynamic therapy was not useful and that supportive therapy was more helpful to the patients in terms of obtaining work. However, only 25% of the patients in either group finished treatment and were evaluated. Most patients avoided the study doctors, perhaps because they insisted that the patients take their medication.

Karon and VandenBos (1981) randomly assigned 'schizophrenic' patients to one of three groups: one group consisted of patients who were given seventy sessions of psychoanalytic psychotherapy (medication was gradually withdrawn); another was simply maintained on medication; and the third was given a combination of psychotherapy and medication. The results showed that the patients receiving psychotherapy were discharged earliest from hospital, their disorders improved and they were able to lead more 'human' lives. Psychotherapy with medication was more efficacious than medication alone but not as effective as the psychotherapy alone. Due to the reduction in hospitalisation and re-hospitalisation, psychotherapy was much less expensive over a four-year period. Unfortunately, decision makers are more interested in saving money within six months than saving money over four or more years. Also, if patients can be denied benefits entirely or lose their job and therefore their insurance as a result of inadequate treatment, the managed care company may consider these economically successful outcomes.

In the 1950's, Karon instituted a policy of psychotherapy for all psychotic reactions in a reformatory for male adolescents. Patients were given psychotherapy sessions without medication for five days before transfer to the state hospital was considered. Psychotherapy was then continued at a minimum of one session per week. During a six month period, no state hospital transfers were necessary. Before and after this six months, patients were transferred to the state hospital, medicated and remained there for an average of two years before they were returned to the reformatory. However, the DSM-IV makes that comparison seem irrelevant. According to the DSM-IV, only 'brief reactive psychoses' occurred during the six months when psychotherapy was available whereas, before and after that period, the state hospital treated true 'schizophrenics' from the same population!

The Vermont Longitudinal Study followed the most 'hopeless' patients for an average of thirty-two years. These included faeces-smearing patients who barely dressed themselves and had forgotten how to tell the time. The lead researcher, Courtenay Harding, reported that 30% of these patients fully recovered. They were employed in work, had a social life, were free from symptoms and did not take any medication. There is little quantitative research on what promotes recovery. Harding questioned certain patients in the above study, "What really made a difference in your recovery?" Some referred to a person who told them that they had a chance to recover. Someone who believed in them translated into hope (Karon, 2001).

Only long-term systematic research has a chance of making a reasonable contribution. After all, patients often need at least a year to feel comfortable with a new therapist.

Types of Therapy

General Therapies

Family therapy and other direct and conditioning therapies started with the early Freudians. They have been shown to be efficacious in reducing relapses (Barrowclough and Tarrier, 1984).

Family Systems model

Family systems have a natural propensity to settle down into patterns that may prove dysfunctional in the long-term. For example, the child may unconsciously adopt an illness or a rebellious streak to deflect his/her parents' attention from their own marital problems. Maladaptive system dynamics are identified and are ideally altered in the Family Systems model so that individuals no longer maintain the problem.

Milieu therapy is where mental hospitals are discarded in favour of social rehabilitation units. Social contact is encouraged and a timetable helps provide a routine. Hogarty et al. (1986) and Liberman et al. (1986) have found improvement in such a setting.

The **Behavioural model** regards symptoms as learned habits or 'maladaptive learned responses'. If these habits are modified, the problems should be eliminated. Confrontational stances are avoided and patients are sensitively questioned about the reason for their abnormal beliefs. Various behaviour therapy techniques have been devised on the basis of the theoretical principles of learning and have been consistently and remarkably effective in treating a range of disorders. For 'schizophrenia', they have been shown to be of benefit in combating hallucinations (Slade and Bentall, 1988). However, this model does not deal with the distress or reasons for the development of symptoms.

A depressed mood might lead to depressed, pessimistic thinking. The **Cognitive model** treats such distortions of thinking as primary, not secondary. If biases in thinking can be corrected and people can be educated out of their false beliefs, they should be less likely to fall into a reciprocal relationship or vicious circle between disturbed thought and disturbed feelings. Johnson et al. (1977) treated a male patient who could not explain certain nocturnal emissions and consequently developed a delusional belief that occult 'warm forms' were sexually molesting him. When this was attributed to his own sexual arousal, his delusions subsided.

Research studies have shown cognitive therapy to be highly effective in reducing symptoms of a wide variety of disorders, including some negative 'schizophrenic' symptoms and attention deficits. Cognitive-behavioural interventions have successfully treated delusions. Hartman and Cashman (1983) treated two males and one female with a combination of psychopharmacological and cognitive-behavioural procedures. The psychological methods effected the greater impact.

The **Humanistic-Existential model** acknowledges the distress caused when there is a large gap between 'the self-image' and 'the ideal self'. The client engages in frank and deep self-exploration and moves towards self-acceptance. The therapy is 'client-centred'. The clients are not termed 'patients', they are in control and there is no diagnosis. Carl Rogers and other humanistic practitioners maintain that "a scientific approach to human affairs is bound to be subject to fundamental distortion and that orthodox psychology provides no more than a shallow, limited and biased account of the experience of being human" (cited in Frude, 1998).

Targeting Positive Symptoms

Operant Procedures

This is a procedure that reinforces patients when they speak in a comprehensive and rational manner. In 1972, Nydegger successfully treated a twenty-year old paranoid 'schizophrenic' who suffered from auditory and visual hallucinations, delusions and social withdrawal. He instructed the patient to treat his voices as thoughts and gave him social approval when he managed to. The patient also received assertion training, systematic desensitisation and verbal conditioning to treat his delusional speech. He displayed immediate relief from his symptoms and this relief was maintained until a subsequent meeting two-and-a-half years later (Bentall, 1990).

Systematic Desensitisation

This reduces stresses associated with the occurrence of hallucinations such as family stress (Slade, 1972). An imaginal desensitisation programme is used. Reductions in tension and frequency of auditory hallucinations have been reported.

Thought Stopping

There are four stages in thought stopping:

1. The therapist instructs the patient to raise his/her index finger every time he/she experiences a hallucination.
2. The patient is then encouraged to replace the raising of the index finger with shouting, 'Stop it!'
3. The patient is then instructed to whisper, 'Stop it!'
4. The patient is finally reduced to thinking, 'Stop it!'

This technique has been successful in two single case studies (Samaan 1975, Johnson et al. 1983). Lamontagne et al. (1983) conducted a controlled trial where twenty patients who had been diagnosed with paranoid 'schizophrenia' and were taking chlorpromazine were randomly assigned to two groups, one of which received thought-stopping treatment in addition to their medication. The group receiving thought-stopping improved on most measures, particularly in relation to paranoid thoughts.

Counter-Stimulation (distraction)

Here, another stimulation is present to drown out the voices. One study (Feder, 1982) instructed a patient suffering from hearing intermittent voices to wear stereo headphones with AM-FM radio. The patient's voices stopped completely at work when wearing the headphones but remained when not wearing them.

Self-Monitoring

The patient keeps an ongoing record of the occurrence and duration of the voices. Four studies have produced positive results. Reybee and Kinch (1973) treated two male chronic 'schizophrenics' using this procedure. When monitoring was carried out retrospectively, there was no reduction in hallucinations but when the patients sat in front of an event-recorder and signalled the start, length and termination of their voices by pressing a button, there was a marked reduction in hallucination frequency in both patients (Bentall, 1990). Acknowledging voices is often the first step in taking control.

Aversion and Punishment Techniques

Electric shocks or white noise are used as aversive stimuli. Weingaertner (1971) randomly assigned patients to a shock group, a pseudoshock group and a non-treatment control group. The former two groups were instructed to press a shock button when they experienced the voices but the pseudoshock group's circuit had been disconnected. All three groups improved in terms of reported frequency of hallucinations but there were no significant differences between groups. A study such as this has ethical considerations. Slade et al. (1986) used white noise but concluded that the therapeutic effects of aversion therapy are due to self-monitoring rather than aversive conditioning.

Ear-Plug Therapy

This was first suggested by Green (1978) and was based on his theory that there is defective interhemispheric transfer of information in 'schizophrenic' patients. The insertion of an ear-plug in the left ear was deemed successful in producing dramatic therapeutic results (James 1983, Morley 1987). However, wearing the ear-plug in the right ear or switching it from one ear to the other has often produced better results. This seems highly erratic.

First-Person Singular Therapy

Greene (1978) believed auditory hallucinations to be internally generated and asserted that sufferers should take control of and accept responsibility for their hallucinations. He reported success using this therapeutic strategy with two female patients, both of whom were relieved of their voices. Fowler (1986) also noted a dramatic reduction in hallucinations in 20% of his patients when using this approach.

Perhaps all of the above are beneficial in treating hallucinations because they operate at a different point on the hallucinatory mechanism, or positive expectations could be generated causing the placebo effect. It seems that the therapies above fit into three categories: self-monitoring, anxiety reduction and distraction procedures.

Although these therapies provide effective coping strategies, the alleviations provided may be short-term because the origins of the hallucinations and delusions have not been explored.

Targeting Negative Symptoms

The Token Economy

This motivates patients to behave appropriately and constructively by giving them tokens whenever they behave in an acceptable manner. It is then possible for the patient to exchange their tokens for treats such as drinks, cigarettes, watching television, etc. This procedure was introduced in large psychiatric hospitals in the USA in the 1960's with positive results. The UK used it in the 1970's with chronic institutionalised patients but with less success. The efficacy of this regime depends on how well it is explained to the patients at the outset and the consistency of the staff. It can be a useful tool to bridge the gap between being in hospital and transferring to live in the community but requires a favourable staff to patient ratio and an overwhelming commitment from all staff. There are also ethical considerations to be made: for example, the patients have to earn privileges that should be available to any adult. However, some patients may benefit from being treated in this way if their own upbringing was dysfunctional.

Social-Skills Training

In the Scale for the Assessment of Negative Symptoms (Andreasen, 1982), affective flattening, anhedonia-asociality and poor attention were regarded as the three negative symptoms which are social in nature. Studies seem to have demonstrated only short-term benefits of this approach (Curran and Monti, 1982) yet patients receiving a combination of social-skills training and family therapy were least likely to relapse over a two-year period (Hogarty et al., 1986).

Life Skills Training

This was administered to chronic 'schizophrenic' patients in a study by Murray Brown (1982). The patients attended a day-patient unit for five days a week for seven weeks. The training modules focused on interpersonal skills, nutrition and meal planning, health and hygiene, managing money, pre-vocational issues and the use of community resources and social networks. The initial outcome was favourable but no follow-up study has been carried out to assess the long-term benefits of this training.

Self-Instructional Training

This teaches patients to control their own behaviour by instructing themselves out aloud and then covertly. Bentall et al. (1987) discovered that the cognitive performance of patients suffering predominantly from negative symptoms improved.

Problem-Solving Approaches

Hansen et al. (1985) conducted a study of six chronic 'schizophrenic' patients. They were trained in a procedure for solving interpersonal problems by identifying their problem, defining a goal, generating a solution, evaluating alternatives and thus selecting the best solution. Beneficial effects were produced, evident at one and four-month follow-ups.

Self-Control of Symptoms

Some individuals develop an awareness of the factors likely to exacerbate their condition and find effective coping strategies. This is perhaps the most pro-active and beneficial way of managing one's symptoms because the patient takes responsibility for his/her own problems. In order for this to happen, the patient must retain enough insight into their situation in the context of normal behaviour and reasoning. This might be ineffective in severe cases.

About two-thirds of patients and their relatives recognise certain 'prodromal' effects, including loss of interest, problems with concentration, disturbing dreams and withdrawal a week or so before the onset of an acute relapse. Thus the psychotic episode may be prevented if they seek help when the above warning signs appear. If certain stress management manoeuvres and reassuring self-statements are employed by the patient, the severity of the prodromal symptoms may be reduced. Worrying about the symptoms may trigger the onset of a full-blown relapse.

One must, if possible, learn to relax, accept the pain and view it as a feeling, not a fact that could threaten one's existence. "What sets me apart from these 'sick' ones is simply a learned ability to manage the blades of deep pain with a little bit of dexterity... I have not healed so much as learned to sit still and wait while pain does its dancing work, trying not to panic or twist in ways that make the blades tear deeper, finally infecting the wounds" (Slater, 1996). In effect, Slater is referring to the fact that sufferers will be more capable of managing pain if they acknowledge its presence rather than avoid it.

Patients have reported that breathing exercises help calm them. Also, taking part in a creative activity such as drama therapy may expand their role repertoires, freeing them from debilitating constraints. It is necessary that patients maintain control, particularly in areas where they might regress to playing previous roles.

No single therapy model would be adequate to treat all 'schizophrenics' as they do not form a homogeneous group. The ideal approach would be for the therapist to cater for the needs of the individual and practise elements of many of the models above at his own discretion.

Chapter 3

Criticisms of Current Procedures

Medication

Neuroleptic drugs were introduced in 1954. It was promised that they would stop this illness called 'schizophrenia' by 1970. However, the only thing they stopped was the development of other forms of treatment. Since their introduction, the professional role has changed from one of pro-activity to one of re-activity or even inactivity. The lack of resources, particularly time, means a high proportion of staff resort to administering medication as it provides a much quicker relief of symptoms in the short-term. This makes the patient dependent in the long-term.

Phil Thomas, a consultant psychiatrist, defines a high dosage of drugs as 'social control'. He found that doctors prescribe more medication when there are fewer staff on duty. High levels of chemicals cause clients to spend much of their time in a drug-induced stupor and often up to twenty hours sleeping per day.

Patients are not given the opportunity to speak for themselves and are frequently offered no alternative treatments to medication. Families and professionals are settling for treatments which aim at making the patient a life-long cripple who is not too disturbing!

Neuroleptic medication reduces hallucinations and other positive symptoms as well as disturbing affect and some of its immediate consequences. It improves some of the patients' behaviour and makes them more compliant. Just because neuroleptics affect psychotic behaviour in ways that many people consider to be desirable (more docile, socially conforming and receptive to further treatment), it does not prove that 'schizophrenia' and other psychotic disorders are organic diseases. A parallel argument would be: Alcohol, a drug, can change normal people's behaviour, sometimes positively and sometimes negatively. Therefore normality is a disease and alcohol is a treatment.

If patients do not appear to improve with medication, it is often perceived that they are failing the medication rather than that the medication is failing them. Psychiatrists often blame the patients' own physiology for the ineffectiveness of the treatment (Coleman, 1999).

Harding (1988) conducted a study of patients who fully recovered from 'schizophrenia'. They were among the 50% of patients who had stopped taking medication.

Docherty (1975) found that only four out of thirty-one studies measured the effectiveness of drug therapy on dimensions other than symptom relapse or re-hospitalisation when reviewing literature. Giving a comprehensive assessment of the patients' functioning is severely limited unless it is based on multiple outcome dimensions. Studies must have longer follow-ups to assess long-term advantages.

If medication is so beneficial to patients, why do they remain actively psychotic in the long-term? It is dangerous and foolish to see medication as anything more than a short-term strategy. It could be used as a transitional object or for symptom relief.

People might need a small dose of medication initially to provide a 'window of calm'. "Whenever medications are used during psychotherapy, their meaning and usefulness to patient and therapist must be continuously scrutinised to prevent medications becoming a vehicle for the unconscious avoidance of the therapeutic task" (Levy, 1993).

Psychological Disadvantages
The enthusiasm for drugs runs a risk of ignoring psychological components that are necessary for effective and humane intervention. A drug that alleviates symptoms still leaves untouched the basic tendency of an individual to react abnormally in stressful situations. Many patients do not improve with anti-psychotic drugs (Crow at al., 1986). Much more must be learned about individual differences.

Medication can make one unable to use the psychological coping methods one has previously used. It can cause a heightening of passivity and feelings of helplessness due to it being regarded as a magical substance. Medication modifies the patient's characteristics and symptoms so that they do not possess the energy required to respond to other forms of treatment. "Neuroleptics may interfere with the schizophrenic's attempt to use external reality, especially interpersonal relationships, to ward off psychotic conflicts and further psychotic disintegration" (Nevins, 1993). One could question patients as to how they can help their psychotic symptoms and build on their existing control mechanisms thus giving them back responsibility. "Some patients may rely on subtle fluctuations in affect and thought to signal symptom evolution that could be obscured by medications, making self-control more difficult" (Breier and Strauss, 1983).

Neuroleptics can interfere with access to primary-process thinking. They can also interrupt hallucinations, grandiose delusions and omnipotent feelings. The 'schizophrenic' may be unable to deal with the sense of loss and narcissistic change. (15) How can the origins of hallucinations and delusions be uncovered if they are reduced to such a substantial degree by medication? Metaphorically, if an individual complains that he has a thorn penetrating his leg and it is causing him pain, pain-killers would not cure that pain. They might dull the intensity of it in the short-term as well as causing numerous side-effects but they will not expel the thorn. The pain is a message to the brain to inform it that the skin needs attention. Taking medication is ignoring this message. In the long term, the wound may turn septic and become more serious. Patients are encouraged to repress and deny their symptoms. Thus their condition will deteriorate because the primary cause of their symptoms is not being investigated or addressed.

Neurological Disadvantages

There have been several reports of an important reaction between dopamine and cholinergic agents thus causing a reverse in the therapeutic effects of neuroleptics in some 'schizophrenics', following the administration of anticholinergics (neuroleptic side-effect combaters). The most notorious irreversible side-effect is 'Tardive Dyskinesia' (a neurological disorder) which causes the patient to make slow, involuntary rhythmical movements of the limbs and continuous oral movements. This disorder also impairs one's ability to speak and eat which will reinforce the patient's already present negative self-image. "One of the problems with medication is that it flattens your emotions. It induces a tranquillity of sorts but this is more like a numbness or hollow feeling...Emotions can be expressed in a positive way without having to suppress everything" (Dave, Hearing Voices, 2001).

Breggin and Cohen's (2000) reviews of the literature on brain-damaging effects of psychiatric medication indicate that the mental health system is creating a population of brain-damaged people. As disadvantages of medication are being learned, some psychiatrists are returning to the use of ECT, perhaps to provoke some affect in their patients that has been flattened by the medication! They refuse to turn to psychotherapy due to having no training in it and its threat of making them, as medical practitioners, redundant. According to a study, psychiatrists whose practice is confined to medication and evaluation can earn $300000 compared to $100000 if they practise only psychotherapy (Moran, 1993).

Mary Moate (1990) said of her son, "He also hated taking his medication, protesting that the tablets made him feel continually tired" (Moate, 1990). The brain is a system with only part localisation of functioning and thus it is only at a theoretical level that one may consider isolating one subsystem from the whole. No drug can solely target the required area.

Azima (1957, 1959) considered drugs to affect drive systems and hence cause the emergence of aggressive impulses.

Olanzapine (a neuroleptic) can cause weight gain which, in turn, can lead to Type 2 diabetes.

Withdrawal

Davis (1975) believes that all patients deserve a trial of withdrawal from medication to enhance their clinical course and reduce the risk of neurological complications. Research points out that if medication is carefully reduced by 40%, therapy can be much more effective.

Many patients improve during the drying-out period. They show more spontaneity, fuller affect, less psychomotor retardation and more social and work initiative. This contradicts the belief that failure to medicate acute 'schizophrenics' is unethical.

Relapse

There are numerous reasons why 'schizophrenic' patients suffer relapses when their symptoms have abated. Relapses depend on the emotional climate in a patient's home or residence and the amount of time he/she spends with certain relatives. Some environments are emotionally intense and are marred by constant harassment, unnecessary demands and undue criticism.

According to Frude (1998), major relapses occur if phenothiazines are discontinued. "Thus patients need to be maintained on medication over the longer term" (ibid.). Long-term use of this drug can cause structural defects in the brain and numerous side-effects: for example, insomnia, muscle trembling, drowsiness and visual disturbances. "Fortunately, most of these side-effects can be controlled by the use of appropriate medication" (Frude, 1998). Frude appears to be recommending an infinite cocktail of drugs to prevent a relapse. Also major tranquillizers lose effectiveness with long-term administration.

Studies seldom include groups who have been free of drugs from the moment of their breakdown and hospitalisation. Therefore there is no data on the relapse rate during the natural course of the 'schizophrenic' process.

Rufus May became 'high' and his thoughts raced when he attempted to wean himself off medication. This was assumed to be a relapse. Breggin wrote that withdrawal symptoms may encourage the doctor and patient to resume the drug prematurely. What is actually required is a period of time where the withdrawal effects can take their natural course. These can include sweating, shivering, vomiting, suffering from insomnia, hearing more voices, experiencing visions and developing paranoia (Coleman, 1999).

Psychiatry

When the Nazis stigmatised and segregated the Jews and when Americans stigmatise and segregate those who have Black skin or Japanese ancestry, it is persecution, but when people stigmatise and segregate their relatives and neighbours who behave in ways the majority of people do not approve of, it is psychiatry (Szasz, 1979).

In the Aboriginal Culture, if someone goes mad, the whole tribe meets to discuss what they have done to cause the person to go mad. In the Western world the professionals meet to discuss what is wrong with the patient. This is an impersonal, rather than person-centred, means of dealing with the problem as the patient is often not considered or even consulted.

Scott (1973) stated that the successful labelling of an individual requires negotiation between three parties: the diagnostic expert, the patient and significant others. The presumed yet highly questionable biological substrate of 'schizophrenia' legitimised the role of medical practitioners in the management role. Psychiatrists view symptoms objectively which takes the individual out of his/her social and cultural context. They must accept that generalisations do not always apply to individuals.

Psychiatrists have claimed too large a territory for themselves. If there was no psychiatry, there could be no 'schizophrenics'. People with problems would not disappear but the stigma would. "Psychiatrists have couched their profession in a scientific language that very few outside the profession can understand. They have shrouded themselves within a discourse that alienates their clients" (Coleman, 1999). Marion Milner's first professor of psychology, C.E. Spearman, said that good psychologists do not use words that are only meaningful to the specialist. Slater (1996) spoke of the rift between practitioners and patients. "This rift is reflected in the language only practitioners are privy to, in words like 'glossolalia' and 'echolalia' instead of just saying 'the music of madness'"(Slater, 1996).

One psychiatrist in America said he lived in constant fear of litigation from patients or their families if anything went wrong. He stated that the best defence was to prove in court that he had actively been treating his client with drugs as laid down by the American Psychiatric Association. In light of the negative side effects of neuroleptic medication mentioned earlier, this is tragic. The Doctor's Hippocratic Oath states, "I will prescribe regimen for the good of my patients according to my ability and my judgement and, above all else, first do no harm." The role of any professional should be to question everything and allow for the opportunity of change, advancements and breakthroughs.

Personal Accounts

Mike, a sufferer of male sexual abuse, was a psychiatrist by profession. "The only source of help I could think of was psychiatry and that idea was instantly placed as a very last resort indeed! I could not imagine any of the psychiatrists with whom I had worked or whom I knew being able to help. After all, I had never come across such a situation in my time working in psychiatry" (Etherington, 2000). This confirms the medical nature of the profession yet mental health problems are never solely biological in nature. Therefore psychiatrists are ill-qualified to treat 'schizophrenics'. They have neither the time nor the experience to practise psychotherapy. In most circumstances, the pressure to prescribe a drug is very great.

The turning point for Rufus May occurred when his friend, Celine, committed suicide shortly after her medication had been increased. She had a "constant tremble and shuffling movement and she was dribbling...These effects were adding to her problems rather than taking away her distress and I just felt that other options hadn't been tried...I've been there. I've been shuffling from foot to foot, dribbling. It's dehumanising...I was suggesting that she needed to negotiate a lower dose but there was a kind of culture, 'a doctor knows best'...I'm sure there were lots of distressing problems she was struggling with but no-one was exploring these with her and that was the key. Madness is when other people choose to stop trying to understand you" (May, 2001).

One mother of a 'schizophrenic' said, "We answered many of the questions of the young interviewing doctor, even though we felt that many of them were of little relevance to us. Still, he was the expert and we were 'at his mercy', so to speak. But we did sense a coolness, an air of indifference almost. I must confess that as we left, I still felt as confused as ever" (Moate, 1990).

Institutionalisation

Themes of dominance, coercion and control are made explicit and pervasive within most medical practices. Neuroleptics are often used as 'chemical strait-jackets'. Noncompliant patients receive the worst and potentially most harmful treatments. They may be locked in seclusion, placed in restraints, chemically and physically strait-jacketed, lobotomised, shocked and beaten. Patients should have the right to take risks and make certain decisions. Otherwise, the whole process is perverted into stabilisation and maintenance at best and incarceration at worst but never growth and development. A person will turn inward because it is the only place where the psychiatric system cannot control him/her.

"Lack of insight is common...it predisposes the individual to noncompliance with the treatment" (DSM-IV, 1994). It is the DSM-IV and many psychiatrists who lack 'insight'! They account for the 10% suicide rate by hospital discharge. Patients become so heavily reliant upon medication and a non-challenging atmosphere that taking responsibility for themselves again is extremely difficult. The way to counteract this is to never relieve them of responsibility in the first place.

"Most people who have worked for any amount of time at a psychiatric facility have witnessed abuses of the diagnostic process. Patients are sometimes assigned labels that are poorly justified...and they will be free of all responsibilities" (Davison and Neale, 1994).

In hospital, patients are often asked to discuss their emotions yet when their feelings are actually expressed, they are met with dismissal, condescension and false interpretations: for example, if one cries, one is suicidal; anger is indicative of aggression and danger; laughter is a sign of mania, thus requiring sedation.

Personal Recollections

Susan, in the case study written by Marion Milner, viewed

mental hospitals as prisons, full of destroyed or injured people, from which she felt she would never again emerge. "It was to be after this stay in hospital that she was to say to me that if I knew as much as she now did about mental hospitals, I would know she would have rotted there if she had gone into one in these earlier years" (Milner, 1969).

Janet Frame felt panic at being locked up. The years passed and the diagnosis remained with no-one apparently questioning it. "I felt hopelessness at my plight. The years that followed...were full of fear and unhappiness, mostly caused by my confinement and treatment in hospital...I now had what was known as a 'history' and ways of dealing with those with a history were stereotyped without investigation...As the months passed by, [I had] to endure that constant state of physical capture where I was at the mercy of those who made judgements and decisions without even talking at length to me or trying to know me...The attitude of those in charge...was that of reprimand and punishment with certain forms of medical treatment being threatened as punishment for failure to co-operate...The swamping wave of horror when an overworked young doctor who had scarcely spoken to me except to ask, 'How are you?' and not wait for a reply now found time to explain that I was to have a leucotomy operation, that it would be good for me" (Frame, 1984). No-one spoke to her for longer than fifteen minutes over a total of eight years.

"Patients kick and scream and fight when they aren't sure the doctor can see them. It's a most terrifying feeling to realise that the doctor can't see the real you and that he's just going ahead with his own ideas. I would start to feel that I was invisible or maybe not there at all. I had to make an uproar to see if the doctor would respond to me, not just to his own ideas" (Joan, cited in Laing, 1959). The doctor would respond by instructing a nurse to administer a higher dose of medication. The way patients are treated often demands deviant behaviour.

Bassman, a psychologist who was once diagnosed and treated

for 'schizophrenia', was told he had an incurable disease called 'schizophrenia'. The doctor told his parents that he would need to take medication for the rest of his life. "The hospital doctor put me into a coma five days a week for eight weeks by injecting me with insulin. Those forty insulin treatments, combined with ECT, blasted huge holes in my memory, parts of which have never returned. I ballooned from 140 to 170 pounds...and the heavy doses of Thorazine and Stelazine made me feel like I was walking in slow-motion under water" (Ronald Bassman, 2001). He initially concealed his past and suffered in silence as he knew this was the only way to succeed as a professional.

Rufus May saw a psychiatrist for a few minutes a week whilst in hospital. When he expressed the wish not to take medication, his trousers were taken down and he was "pinned down by five or six nurses who injected it into his backside" (May, 2001). He felt sedated for days afterwards and slept for a high proportion of the time but still felt utterly confused.

Ron Coleman was diagnosed as 'schizophrenic' in less than an hour. "The psychiatric system, far from being a sanctuary and a system of healing, was like a system of fear and continuation of illness for me...It was not until I left the system that the recovery process really got underway in my life" (Coleman, 1999). He spoke of the system having no expectation of the in-patients' recovery, the emphasis being on maintenance. The journey to illness was far too rapid and easy yet the journey to recovery was viewed as almost impossible. The system, he said, taught him how to be a good 'schizophrenic'!

Anne Kraus, a psychiatric survivor working in the mental health field in New York, remembered listening to a female patient complaining angrily that she was not receiving appropriate treatment. At this point, a psychiatrist placed himself between the two ladies with his back to the patient and said, "You know, some people should not be angry with those who are trying to help them. They would get along much better if they showed more respect." After he walked away, the patient ignored Kraus and began talking to the voices she could hear.

A social worker who had the power to section his clients was vacating his position and had the courage to state that he would never want anyone in his family to be forced into psychiatric treatment (Mellor, 2005).

Crow Holbeche, an artist, who recently died of cancer, stated that he would rather be in a hospice dying of cancer than in Wonford House, a psychiatric hospital, without cancer.

Electro-Convulsive Therapy (ECT)

ECT is a barbaric approach to treating human beings. It may cause structural defects (Reveley, 1985) and, like psychosurgery (prefrontal lobotomy), has proved to be basically ineffective for 'schizophrenia'. The known adverse effects of ECT include death, brain damage, memory loss, seizures, suicide and personality changes (Breggin 1997, Morgan 1999).

Personal Recollections

Susan complained that she "lost her soul," was "no longer there" and had "no feelings" since her ECT (Milner, 1969). She also observed other patients who looked peaceful as if dead. Her doctor recommended that she have ECT if she saw things looking fuzzy. Surely this could have been a side-effect of her medication.

Coleman endured forty sessions of ECT and was forcibly medicated even though it gave him no respite. His voices remained as virulent as ever.

Janet Frame was discharged from hospital after two hundred applications of unmodified ECT. A few years hence when she was cataloguing medical papers in the brain museum, she learned that ECT was commended as a means of provoking fear in the patient.

Diagnosis of 'Schizophrenia' and the DSM-IV (1994)

The earliest versions of the DSM were significantly influenced by psychoanalytic thinking. Neurosis was included as a major category. This aetiological focus has mostly been abandoned in the recent manuals. Each condition is now defined in terms of observable symptoms. The DSM is seen as a useful diagnostic aid and identifies a wide range of clinical conditions.

'Schizophrenia' is very poorly defined in literature even though Morel, Kraepelin, Bleuler, Schneider and Langfeldt have classified and re-classified the symptoms and characteristics of 'schizophrenia', as has the American Psychiatric Association. It is vital that the condition is demystified. Some psychiatrists place too much emphasis on the diagnosis of a patient - "Hence the relief of a firm diagnosis given by an expert because it does, though only particularly, explain the disturbed behaviour of the patient" (Enoch, 1990). A diagnosis cannot explain a patient's behaviour. Even the patient may be unable to explain his/her behaviour due to repression. A diagnosis merely informs a patient that they suffer from a certain collection of symptoms.

Moral Considerations

Diagnosis affects the life of the patient, his/her family and defines the sort of treatment the patient receives. Despite the progress made in the field of human rights, a diagnosis of psychosis continues to be a serious social handicap.

The DSM approach inappropriately medicalises psychological distress. It seems particularly unsuitable to include 'partner relational problems' and 'sexual abuse of a child' as 'conditions'. Chemical changes in the brain may be the effects of psychological processes: for example, the tragic death of a loved one. It would be highly inappropriate to regard the bereaved party as suffering from a biological disorder. Human beings are much more than organisms who are at the mercy of their genetic neurochemistry.

An exclusively biological perspective on mental disorder leads us to forget that sufferers remain people. In some branches of medicine, even today, patients are referred to as 'clinical material'. Referring to somebody as a person rather than a diagnosis is imperative. It constantly reinforces the fact that one is treating a real human being, not just a medical label. Professor Robin Murray (Head of General Psychiatry, Institute of Psychiatry, London) stated that the 'schizophrenia' label is unhelpful as it can act as a barrier to receiving the correct treatment at the correct time. He also said that if he was diagnosed with 'schizophrenia', he would ask for another doctor (Bhugra and Bahl, 1999).

One must disregard the static approach of mathematics: 2A+3B=C and aim to describe the phenomena in a kinematic, developmental way: If A or B, then C, then D. One must be fascinated with realness rather than orderliness. "It is a sad reflection on western society that, rather than valuing the range a person can display in their being, one's very sanity depends upon the predictability and social acceptability of being 'a type'" (Chadwick, 1997).

Reliability and Validity

A diagnostic system must be reliable and valid. One cannot guarantee that a reliable system is valid but an unreliable system must be invalid (Spitzer and Fliess, 1974). One psychiatrist's perception of 'schizophrenia' must be identical to another's for the diagnosis to be meaningful. Though the term 'schizophrenia' has been generally adopted by psychiatrists, two from the same medical school cannot agree on who is 'schizophrenic' independently of one another for more than 80% of cases. Agreement is even less in different schools and countries (Laing and Esterson, 1964).

Early studies (as above) demonstrated that psychiatrists were inconsistent in their assigning of individuals to diagnostic criteria (Beck et al. 1962, Blashfield 1973) so they now operate structured interviews for patients and use operational criteria for different psychiatric diagnoses. These are contained in the DSM and the PSE (Present State Examination), developed by Wing et al. (1974). A higher frequency of agreement in diagnoses between psychiatrists has thus been fostered. However, acceptable levels of concordance were only achieved between Schneider's criteria and the PSE diagnosis which was actually constructed using Schneider's description of 'schizophrenia'. There is also such a wide diversity between Schneider's criteria and the DSM-III criteria that one patient could be considered 'schizophrenic' using one but not the other.

If two or more psychiatrists arrive at the same diagnosis, it does not guarantee the validity of the diagnosis. Often, additional evidence that emerges later may contradict the diagnosis. However, the psychiatrist may not admit that his original diagnosis was initially wrong and so refuse to alter it. Diagnoses should be treated as working hypotheses and should be re-examined throughout the course of clinical intervention and assessment.

Reliability

The reliability of a diagnostic system refers to the consistency with which subjects are classified. There is a poor correlation between symptoms and diagnoses of 'schizophrenia'. Delusions are experienced by 'schizophrenic' and 'affective' patients; thought disorder is a symptom of 'schizophrenia', 'depression', 'aphasia' and 'mania'; and hallucinations are experienced by patients with a wide range of conditions. The cognitive dysfunctions found in 'schizophrenics' have also been found in patients with other diagnoses.

If psychiatric disorders are discrete, there should be relatively few patients suffering from the symptoms of more than one disorder. Otherwise the characterisations are meaningless. Slade and Cooper (1979) discovered that hospitalised patients are likely to suffer more symptoms than out-patients and therefore inflate the association between symptoms.

To overcome uncertainty, the American Psychiatric Association (1980) introduced 'schizotypal personality disorder' to denote individuals who show some but not a sufficient degree of the symptomatology required for a diagnosis of 'schizophrenia'. "A diagnosis of 'Psychotic Disorder Not Otherwise Specified' may be made if insufficient information is available to choose between 'Schizophrenia' and other psychotic disorders" (DSM-IV, 1994). The DSM-IV even describes an Undifferentiated Type of 'Schizophrenia', a residual category! The pressure to establish a working diagnosis means psychiatrists will tend to focus on those diagnoses which they believe to be most likely. Cases are assigned to categories without differentiating between the different degrees of a condition.

In a study by Everitt et al. (1971), over 60% of patients fell into two or three 'dustbin' clusters containing patients with almost every type of diagnosis. It seems that the introduction of diagnoses such as 'schizo-affective disorder' might be an attempt to categorise those who fall into more than one category but this process of re-naming does nothing to help the sufferers.

Bagshaw and McPherson (1978) and Sturt (1981) accepted that a significant number of patients diagnosed as psychotic also experience neurotic symptoms (Bentall, Jackson and Pilgrim, 1988). Therefore the borderline between neurosis and psychosis is arbitrary in nature. "The popular notion of psychotic nucleus, along with the attempt to fix new intermediary categories or to re-awaken older ones - borderlines, psychopaths, narcissistic or schizoid personalities etc. - implies a continuous series, from psychosis to neurosis, that exists without real borders. Diagnosis, thus, becomes secondary" (Soler, publication date unavailable). However, Lacan was adamant about the differentiation between psychosis and neurosis and considered the diagnosis to be imperative.

At the end of the observation on the Schreber case, Freud traced out a watershed between paranoia and paraphrenia. He divided the field of psychosis in two and stated that "when a paranoiac was far too paranoid, he would end up deluding" (1911). "There's a continuum between what we see as 'mental health' and 'confusing ideas' and we all slide along it...If we medicalise it and pigeon hole it, we're only going to breed misunderstanding which is dangerous" (May, 2001).

Any method of classification should take the continuum that exists between psychotic and non-psychotic experiences into account. A successful system would require the analysis of symptom data collected from a wide range of people living in the community enabling psychotic and non-psychotic mental processes to be linked. Not everybody is completely sick and not everybody is completely well.

"It seems that a categorical approach to the description and understanding of psychopathology - the assumption that forms of madness can be subdivided into discrete diagnostic groups (eg. DSM-III R) - must be rejected as scientifically and practically useless" (Bentall, 1990). The DSM-IV rationalises bad treatment. The very same symptom picture is diagnosed as 'brief reactive psychosis', 'schizophreniform psychosis' or 'schizophrenia', solely dependent on whether the patient recovers in less than one month, more than one month but less than six months or more than six months, irrespective of the type or inadequacy of treatment.

The actual experiences and conduct of patients should be the main starting point. One should remain neutral with respect to the environment/biology debate. Diagnoses should be abandoned and the causes for individual symptoms investigated (Bannister 1968, Harvey and Neale 1983, Bentall et al. 1988). It would be more effective to formulate a manual which lists symptoms individually, the possible causes and the best therapies for these. Persons (1986) identified five advantages of symptom-oriented research: it avoids problems of diagnosis and classification; it focuses on phenomena usually ignored; it facilitates theoretical development; it recognises that clinical phenomena are related to normal behaviour; and it may improve classification systems due to a better understanding of individual symptoms being achieved.

Validity

Validity refers to the meaningfulness and utility of the diagnostic categories. For the concept to be valid, a person suffering from one symptom should have a high probability of suffering from other symptoms. However, any two 'schizophrenic' patients may have no symptoms in common (Bannister, 1968). The diagnosis should predict outcome and a characteristic response to treatment. This only appears so for the research on excess dopamine production and the effectiveness of neuroleptic drugs (dopamine blockers). The diagnosis should also bear some relation to aetiology. However, the cause of 'schizophrenia' is questionable.

In the DSM-IV it states that the negative symptoms of 'schizophrenia' "may be due to a variety of other factors (consequence of positive symptoms, medication side effects (16), a mood disorder, environmental understimulation or demoralisation)" (DSM-IV, 1994).

Side effects of medication, understimulation and demoralisation are all consequences of being institutionalised. Negative symptoms persist even when the positive ones are diminished through drugs. Also, motor abnormalities (a positive symptom) "are likely to be related to side effects from treatment with antipsychotic medications" (DSM-IV, 1994).

Only this and one other positive symptom are enough to warrant a diagnosis of 'schizophrenia'. As the negative symptoms, motor disorder and disorganised speech (see 'Medication' above) are also results of medication and institutionalisation, it could be argued that hallucinations and delusions (17) are the only primary symptoms of 'schizophrenia'. (18) It is thus a grave error to declare negative symptoms sufficient to satisfy a diagnosis of 'schizophrenia' if they persist for at least six months.

Rosenhan (1973) conducted a study using eight psychologically healthy people, including himself, who falsely complained of hearing a voice saying 'empty', 'dull' and 'thud' to psychiatrists at various hospitals. All were admitted and seven out of the eight were diagnosed as 'schizophrenic'. During their stay, they wrote down their observations and this was considered symptomatic of the illness. Although they spent nineteen days in hospital, none were detected as impostors. Their normal activities were viewed as abnormal and consequently they were not treated as capable human beings. This demonstrates that mental health professionals may find it impossible to distinguish between psychiatric patients and healthy people. It also contradicts the thorough standard procedure for diagnosing 'schizophrenia' described here by Dr. Enoch: "In order to reach the correct diagnosis of 'schizophrenia', the doctor must adhere to certain clinical procedures. A detailed history must be taken from the patient and from an informed relative, followed by a full physical and mental state examination. The patient might well have to be seen and examined on more than one occasion and the doctor would have to interview other independent witnesses of the disturbed behaviour and change in personality" (Enoch, 1990).

In one case, a psychiatrist asked a 'schizophrenic' if he heard a voice. The patient thought this ridiculous as he could hear the psychiatrist's voice. When asked what the voice was saying to him, the patient replied, "You are a fool," implying that the psychiatrist was a fool. However, this patient was diagnosed as paranoid and suffering from persecutory delusions (Laing, 1959).

The DSM-IV considers the psychotic phenomenon as a 'deficit' (disorder), rather than a production. Freud believed that the psychotic phenomenon was a production and he illustrated this in his analysis of the Schreber case. "A clinic of production (as opposed to a clinic of the deficit) is an indispensable conceptual component of psychoanalytic treatment" (Freud, 1911). An emphasis on the deficit implies a malfunction or disorder and can ignore the order present in every psychopathological structure.

From a Lacanian perspective, a correct diagnosis requires a structural mapping of the subject as well as an adequate description of his/her condition. It is thus possible to make sense of phenomenological manifestations of any given case (1993). He treats the observable phenomena as moments of the structure. "The logical confusions inherent in the concept of schizophrenia are one side effect of the general attempt to subsume behavioural disorders under a framework imported from medicine...The logical usability of the concept of schizophrenia seems to have been little improved by tendencies to hybridise it (schizoaffective, pseudoneurotic schizophrenia), to adjectivise it (schizoid, schizophreniform) or to distribute it (with schizophrenic features, schizophrenic reaction)...To transmute the concept of schizophrenia into a 'phenomenon' or a 'field of study' merely brushes our intellectual troubles under the carpet" (Bannister, 1968).

Forthcoming research must not depend on the current methods of psychiatric classification. The existence of the DSM leads psychiatrists to assess whether or not a person has a particular illness. In other words, a person suffers from 'schizophrenia' or he/she does not suffer from 'schizophrenia'. If one describes a colour as 'not green', this colour could be an infinite number of other colours within the spectrum. Human beings do not fit into categories. No person can live through identical experiences, have identical genetic make-up or possess the same impulses, fantasies and drives as another. The DSM cannot possibly categorise an infinite number of disorders. Therefore it is inadequate.

"Both the fanatical believers and the fixed-attitude people are loud in their scorn of what they call 'woolly minds'... Being woolly, it has no hard edges. It is easy, pliant, yet it has its own toughness. Because it bends, it does not break... The woolly mind realises that we live in an unimaginable, gigantic, complicated, mysterious universe. To try to stuff the vast bewildering creation into a few neat pigeon-holes is absurd. We don't know enough, and to pretend we do is mere intellectual conceit. The best we can do is to keep looking out for clues for anything that will light us a step or two into the dark" (Priestley, cited in Casement, 1990).

Chapter 4

Alternative Explanations for 'Schizophrenia'

Childhood Abuse

In Britain today, one in four females and one in six males have been sexually abused before the age of eighteen (Survivors Swindon, 2001/2). Many 'schizophrenics' have spoken about incest, sexual and physical abuse but such talk has often been dismissed as the ravings of lunatics. However, therapists and researchers who have worked with 'schizophrenics' have reported that the abuse related by those patients was real. "Like society at large, a victim's family and, frequently enough, clients themselves, counsellors and supervisors do not want to know that the people sitting before them were violated sexually - sometimes in sadistic ways - and at a very young age" (Davies and Frawley, 1984, cited in Etherington, 2000).

In childhood abuse, the child becomes overstimulated and overwhelmed and his ego capacity is rendered inoperative. If the abuser is a member of the child's family, the child loses the secure base normally provided by the parents. If the child revealed the abuse, the entire family structure on which the child depends would be threatened and, consequently, his very existence. His efforts to preserve his dependence on his parents for emotional and physical care cause his ego to be separated in two. No verbal link exists between the two dissociated aspects of the self because the child cannot reveal his trauma. However, the body speaks its own language (psychosomatic or even 'schizophrenic' symptoms) and this can be a starting point.

Goleman emphasised how control plays a large part in how effectively an individual can cope. The element of helplessness makes a given event subjectively overwhelming. Because society is intolerant of male helplessness and powerlessness, a boy may rationalise that the dysfunctional sexual relationship is actually positive. He may thus adopt the passive side of the power dynamic in other subsequent adult relationships. Any negative feelings will be repressed, dissociated and denied. In order to survive, the child adapts to his conditions.

Etherington often felt angry, frustrated and de-skilled in the presence of abused patients. However, she used the countertransference as a tool to mirror the patients' feelings back to them. This enabled the patients to reconnect with themselves and then with her. She often provided a language for them and taught them to connect words like 'fear' with the sensation of fluttering in the stomach. Eventually the clients were able to find the correct words to describe their feelings.

If one can delve into the past to find the emotion that connects with the felt sense, there can be a true experiencing and release of emotions. Each feeling (eg. anger, shame, guilt, disgust, contempt, fear, sadness) must be made conscious, separate from the others and labelled correctly. Because abuse and shame are embedded within certain contexts and scenes, the actual scenes must be reactivated. Raine (1999) explained that "re-enactments are emotionally driven attempts to master the overwhelming too-muchness of the traumatic experience. The compulsion to re-live is an attempt to master the terror, helplessness and rage of 'mortal danger'" (Etherington, 2000).

The full imprint of the abuse must be made fully conscious by using metaphor (19), activating imagery, visualisation, stories and poetry which link the sensory processes with cognition and feelings. Etherington suggested that her client, Mike: 'the adult' and 'the child', correspond through writing letters in order for him to engage with himself as an abused little boy.

Oscar, a catatonic 'schizophrenic', drew a picture of his mother and said, "I am afraid of when she dies. Who will take care of me?...It is why I have Sheba and the girls in my head. The crazy thoughts are better than nothing" (Slater, 1996). His father, who was part of a huge child-pornography ring, molested him nightly, took photos of him and filmed him with twenty-five other boys. "It hurts to move because too much is happening. Too much comes in...I can't taste a thing, you know...And it's because, when I was two, my father dropped me from a tree. He stole my taste buds, popping them off my tongue. Later on, I had an operation with a drill before the fire. My body always buzzes. I can't feel nothing" (cited in Slater, 1996). This statement implies that catatonic 'schizophrenia' is a response to suffering the trauma of horrific abuse.

Post-Traumatic Stress Disorder (PTSD)

1% of the population is likely to be affected by PTSD. This diagnosis is less stigmatising than 'schizophrenia' because it acknowledges the reason for a person's odd behaviour. It does not imply that there is something innately wrong with the person. However, some survivors have objected to the use of the term 'disorder' because they see such reactions as entirely normal and understandable in the face of abnormal events. The label effectively amounts to a recognition that any events and social conditions beyond our control may cause extremely disturbing psychological symptoms.

PTSD is found among those who have been exposed to prolonged traumatic circumstances such as childhood sexual abuse. Treatment may progress at a much slower rate and may be fraught with much more complexity than with other traumatised patients who have suffered a single discrete traumatic event. Events that involve actual or threatened death or threat to the physical integrity of a person may produce a more severe effect. The person's response might involve intense fear, helplessness, horror or complete violation. The trauma would be subjectively experienced as extreme. Some assume that those who remain conscious throughout the trauma suffer more acutely than those who become unconscious. This is logical yet it is possible for a person to be physically conscious yet be split-off from their outer body. (20) Events where there is no personal intent to harm produce less severe PTSD.

The cause of PTSD is primarily the event, not the person. However, many people encounter traumatic life events but do not develop PTSD. According to Kessler et al. (1995), 75% of the population have experienced extreme trauma. 33% of the population are debilitated in the long-term (Scott and Palmer, 2000). 46% of 'schizophrenics' were exposed to a traumatic event in the three weeks preceding being given a diagnosis. (21) It is the length and nature of the event and nature of the person's psyche that determine whether or not they will suffer from PTSD. However, some severe external traumas would produce damaging effects on any person, even if the interpretation of them varied (eg. paedophiliac abuse).

The subject's disposition is the key. No-one is endowed with a uniform psychological constitution because of factors such as variation in the strength of drives and strength or weakness of ego-functioning. One must account for the possibility of pre-morbid characterologic vulnerability. A pre-'schizophrenic' suffers the same social and interpersonal stress as do others but the meaning to him and his mode of resolution may differ due to constitutional differences in his psychic make-up, which take shape in the context of his early object relations (relations with: people, eg. parents (Freud); or objects, eg. the breast (Klein)). "Just as in a picture of an egg we recognise every egg we ever saw, so each pain we experience is, in part, built up of all the pains we have ever had" (Szasz, 1962). The things we fear most have already happened to us.

Symptoms

PTSD is characterised by three symptoms: clusters of intrusion, avoidance and disordered arousal. Sufferers have difficulty concentrating (a function of the intrusive images) and an exaggerated startle response. They often exhibit impulsive behaviour, dissociation and adopt obsessional defences like alcohol or drugs. Taking medication thus reinforces this type of defence. Medication cannot ameliorate core PTSD intrusive symptoms (Scott and Palmer, 2000).

Sufferers are often unable to manage basic self-care and they cannot distinguish the past from the present. They are often unable to experience loving feelings because they cannot mourn and may suffer panic attacks, bouts of aggression and unrelenting exhaustion. They often feel guilty and responsible for the event, sometimes even suicidal.

'Numbing' refers to decreased interest in others, a detachment, a sense of estrangement and an inability to feel positive. The person actually oscillates between numbing and re-experiencing the event. (22) Memories of the event(s) may be repressed because they are too painful to repeatedly experience. The individual constantly resorts to psychic numbing and alternates between extreme passivity and rage. He engages in an internal struggle to integrate the trauma into his existing beliefs about himself and the world in an attempt to make sense of it.

"PTSD patients are stuck in time and are continually re-exposed to the traumatic event through daytime recollections that persistently interrupt ongoing thoughts, actions or feelings...During such episodes they find themselves fighting off rapists, being attacked by enemies or fleeing from explosions with the same intense feelings they experienced during the initial trauma" (Scott and Palmer, 2000). They may appear, to an outsider, to be hallucinating. Those who suffer from PTSD endure terrifying nightmares, are scared to go back to sleep and cannot tolerate their memories as they trigger fear, guilt, rage and psychotic episodes. Dreams are recurrent and their content aligns with the traumatic exposure either in original or symbolic form (Scott and Palmer, 2000).

There is ample evidence that extensive development of the frontal lobes (23) is required for memories. A memory may be burned into the brain's emotional computer and alarm system, the amygdala, with such force that dramatic bodily reactions may be triggered and the person may re-experience the precipitating trauma, complete with full sensory replay. The amygdala can store unconscious memories so the person has no explanation of the sensations (eg. palpitations) they are experiencing. Reality dissolves into the reality of the event(s).

Their lack of trust in others and hypervigilance could be perceived as paranoia or, in a more extreme form, catatonia. Excessive attention or extreme alertness to external stimuli, beyond that required for a given realistic appraisal of the level of external threat, may be exhibited. They may demonstrate inappropriate sexual behaviour, suffer from visual and auditory hallucinations, feel permanently damaged and threatened, lose their previously sustained beliefs, change their previous personality characteristics and have fragmented thought processes. One's core beliefs can be violated and invalidated. Someone who has suffered sexual abuse may re-iterate the perpetrator's view of themselves and perceive themselves as 'damaged goods'.

There is a significant amount of overlap between symptoms seen in PTSD and 'schizophrenia' (numbing/flattening of affect, fragmented thought process/thought disorder, re-exposure to trauma/hallucinations, facial grimaces). Among cohorts of treatment-seeking PTSD patients, up to 80% have at least one additional psychiatric diagnosis (Jordan et al., 1991). "Some PTSD patients may be totally incapacitated by this disorder and may appear to have a chronic mental illness. Such patients may be misdiagnosed as having chronic schizophrenia and may be indistinguishable from such patients" (Scott and Palmer, 2000).

Therapy

The therapist must help the patient identify current life situations that trigger traumatic memories to help relieve their symptoms. Therapists should discourage avoidance. "As people have known for many, many years, in order for individuals to come to terms with fearsome happenings, to loose themselves from the hold that events can have over them, they must return to the events and expose themselves fully" (Davison and Neale, 1994).

Winnicott described the patient's need to be able to experience in the present, in relation to a real situation between patient and therapist, the extremes of feeling which belonged to an early traumatic experience which had been 'frozen' because they had been too intense for the primitive ego to encompass at that time (1958). However, patients are generally reluctant to feel and discuss traumas because of the emotional pain involved.

Defence mechanisms can be disadvantageous when therapy commences. One learns to cope and reaches a new equilibrium with the trauma. Metaphorically, one prefers to hobble rather than feel the pain of a back operation. "Trauma memories are, as it were, on an elastic band - the more you push them away, the harder they spring back and you get more injured in the end. Ultimately the band snaps and you snap at yourself and others" (Scott and Palmer, 2000). Unless one can experience the agony leading to psychic death in pain and desolation and journey right into the depths of loss, one can never become real.

When traumatised patients put their experiences into words, it is a critical feature of the healing process. However, the first information given is only the tip of the iceberg. Pennebaker (1986) reported that "those subjects who had an opportunity to write or talk about upsetting events improved their long-term immune functioning, lowered their autonomic nervous system activity, reduced visits to their physician, and evidenced improvement on self-reports of adjustment" (cited in Scott and Palmer, 2000).

The patient is encouraged to tell the story in as much detail as possible including smells, tactile sensations, sounds, what they saw and heard as well as their reactions of horror and disgust. The entire memory must be articulated in words or drawn in a picture to capture parts of the experiences that may be unassimilated. Gaining perspective on events and developing closure regarding stressors can happen when accounts are given. Thoughts and feelings can become more organised, more integrated and less fragmented. One can reframe and reach a degree of acceptance about oneself.

Freud regarded the primary trauma as stimulus flooding. He believed that stimulation causes pain and there is a tendency in the psyche to decrease stimulation in order to decrease pain. He also proposed that every hysteria is the result of a traumatic experience, one that cannot be integrated into the person's understanding of the world. The emotions appropriate to the trauma are not expressed in a direct fashion but are expressed in behaviours that offer a response to the trauma. Thus the symptoms are meaningful. When the patient can be made aware of the meanings of his/her symptoms, the unexpressed emotions are released and no longer need to express themselves as symptoms. Although he only alluded this theory to hysteria, it seems that it is relevant to 'schizophrenia' as severe trauma is implicated.

Hypnotism was successfully used with World War II victims. Horowitz (1988, 1990) used a psychodynamic approach and encouraged patients to discuss their trauma. Discussions of defences and analyses of transference reactions by the patients were also involved.

The Counting Method was developed by Ochberg in 1993 and involves re-telling and re-experiencing the traumatic memories within one hundred counts. The memories tend to be at their most emotionally charged phase during the forties, fifties and sixties. Although they are still present in the nineties, the therapist encourages a winding down period before reaching one hundred. This causes the patient to endure a brief dose of recollection. The memories are thus controlled and connected to the therapist's voice. After the session, the clinician and patient discuss, reframe and digest the traumatic memories and how they were modulated during the counting session. This method ameliorates traumatic experiences (Scott and Palmer, 2000).

Psychophysiological Studies of Trauma

Psychophysiological studies strongly indicate a low threshold of emotional arousal in the 'schizophrenic'. There is also a repeated finding that once aroused, 'schizophrenics' show a retarded rate of recovery from an affective imbalance than do normals. Overleaf, shown by the single and double black lines, is Mednick's "Depiction of Arousal and Recovery Following Stress Onset" (Mednick, Schulsinger, Higgens and Bell, 1968).

The single black line shows a normal person who encounters a stressful situation and quickly recovers. The double black line shows a 'schizophrenic' whose arousal level is originally higher than the normal person's. This could be due to any of the factors listed in Chapter 2. For example, some would propose that the time scale begins at zero and that the 'schizophrenic' is born with a greater sensitivity to external events. Others would hypothesise that environmental considerations, preceding the start of the time scale, have produced such a disposition. The arousal level of the 'schizophrenic' in the face of stress reaches a considerably higher extreme than the normal's and it takes a much longer time for the 'schizophrenic' to recover back to his/her original state. The dotted black line is my own addition and reflects a situation where the 'schizophrenic' continues to suffer stresses or traumas (eg. habitual sexual abuse), represented by each crest on the graph, is not permitted to address the traumas and is plied with medication. When a trauma is not acknowledged or attended to, defences are built up so the person is constantly aroused, expecting the next trauma to occur. "My own journey to illness, far from being a series of biological or chemical events was, in simple words, the culmination of personal life events that I had never dealt with" (Coleman, 1999).

Anticipating the trauma (shown by a positive gradient on the graph) can be even more painful than the occurrence of the trauma (crest) itself. The person begins to prepare themselves for the next trauma and thus they are permanently aroused. I consider the place where the dotted line is almost horizontal to be the place where the person begins to demonstrate typical 'schizophrenic' symptoms, such as lack of affect, and is thus diagnosed.

Mednick believes that the patient creates a repertoire of irrelevant and tangential thoughts to avoid the anxiety. These thoughts will assume the status of a conditioned response which will be elicited automatically when an anxiety producing stimulus is encountered. Eventually the patient will experience less and less anxiety (flattening of affect). This avoidant response should be prevented by psychodynamic psychotherapy (eg. flooding), not physically by medication.

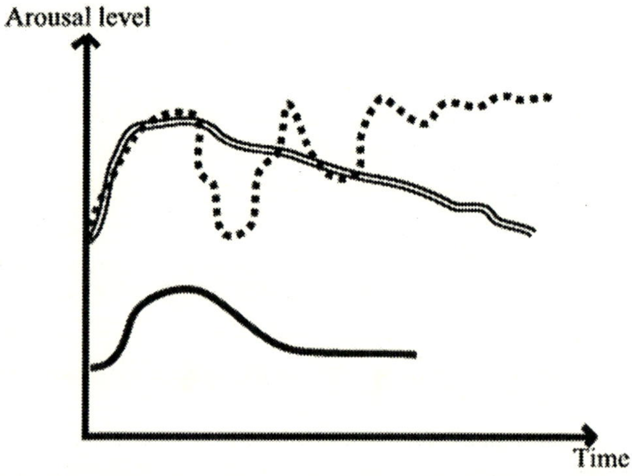

According to Mednick, if stresses continue, the anxiety or arousal level will increase and will affect the 'schizophrenic's learned fear reactions. The increase in breadth of generalisation will cause new stimuli to be interpreted as anxiety arousers and will intensify the reaction to the previously elicited anxiety reactions. Therefore the number of anxiety arousing stimuli increases as does the magnitude of his response to such stimuli. This will in turn increase his anxiety level and hence his generalisation responsiveness.

Consequently, his perception will be distorted through stimulus generalisation. Noises in the plumbing might sound like speech, and shadows may resemble people. Hence he will imagine that he is mentally ill which will cause further anxiety. His psychophysiological state will produce external stimuli which partially cue ongoing thought processes. A rational solution or explanation will be sought and eventually discovered as to why he is so anxious. This attempt at justifying his fears will justify the anxieties and cause atypical behaviours. Hence there is a likelihood of him being diagnosed with paranoid 'schizophrenia'.

Laing's Theory of Schizophrenia

Laing, Szasz and Scheff proposed a fresh outlook on 'schizophrenia' in the 1960's and early 1970's. However, their arguments have mostly now become discredited.

Some 'schizophrenics' fear love as much as they fear hate (Nasar, 1998). They armour themselves against rejection by retreating into a fantasy world or by adopting a hard shell of indifference (Laing, 1959). 'Schizoprenia's "consequence seems to be a frightened sense of isolation and a keen desire to connect, finding fusion through fantasy, the only way the illness knows how" (Slater, 1996).

In Laing's first book, "The Divided Self" (1959), he defined a new theory of 'schizophrenia' and aimed to make madness comprehensible. He argued that a psychotic experiences an acute division between the body and mind, the inner or 'true' self being relegated to a disembodied mind which becomes the spectator of the behaviour of the 'false' self located in an unfeeling, mechanised body. The well-intentioned actions of the therapist or others may be perceived as threatening to this disembodied self which protects its perilous autonomy by severing itself from relation to others and functions primarily through observation and fantasy. Thus the behaviour of the 'schizophrenic' becomes a text which must be decoded by the therapist using his knowledge, understanding and empathy. (24) If the therapist risks interpreting this text, he is drawing upon his own psychotic potentiality to enter into the patient's alien world and is engaging in a human relationship with him/her. This can only happen if the therapist transcends the barriers between professional persona and patient and becomes a person without the armour of theory or the sword of status. (25) Laing maintained that, in an appropriately supportive environment, a 'schizophrenic' would eventually pass safely through the acute phases of his journey. Shock treatments and surgery would only disrupt the natural healing process.

The divorce of the self from the body is one of the basic means of defence for a 'schizophrenic'. The self is afraid to lodge in the body due to an intense fear that it will be subject to attack yet it longs to be embedded in the body. The attempt to kill the self may be undertaken intentionally and is partly defensive. (26) The most extreme defensive posture is that of no longer fearing being crushed, engulfed or overwhelmed by realness because one is already dead. This is perceived by psychiatrists to be 'flattening of affect' or 'catatonia'.

Thus the inner self becomes split, loses its own identity and becomes imprisoned whilst being safe. The inner self is then persecuted by split parts of itself or by its own phantoms which may be uncontrollable. The speech and actions of a 'schizophrenic' become more intelligible and comprehensible if this split into a disembodied self and a body shell is considered. Also, many mental processes will be severed from the self causing fantasy, in-cohesiveness and lack of vitality. "In its final form, such complete disintegration is a hypothetical state which has no verbal equivalents" (Laing, 1959) and its extreme form is incompatible with life.

It is the bizarreness and incomprehensibility that causes extreme difficulty in engaging with a 'schizophrenic'. The complexity and obscurity demonstrated by the individual is often a defence to preserve the privacy of the self against intrusion or further anticipated attack. Any form of understanding threatens their whole defence system. "The schizophrenic is not going to reveal himself for casual inspection and examination to any philandering passer-by. If the self is not known, it is safe. If the schizophrenic is incognito, his body can be handled and manipulated, petted, caressed, beaten, given injections, but 'he', an onlooker, is inviolable" (Laing, 1959). Conversely, the self longs for someone who will accept the true whole person.

This hypothesis of splitting into two is confirmed in many sufferers' accounts of abuse: "If you had actually screwed me it would have wrecked everything. It would have convinced me that you were only interested in pleasure with my animal body and that you didn't really care about the part that was a person...It would have meant you could only see my body and couldn't see the real me which was still a little girl. The real me would have been up on the ceiling watching you do things with my body...When you feed a girl, you make her feel that both her body and her self are wanted. This helps her get joined together. When you screw her she can feel that her body is separate and dead. People can screw dead bodies, but they never feed them" (Joan, a recovered 'schizophrenic', cited in Laing, 1959). The more abuse a person suffers, even if it is the type that happens in institutions, the more the action of splitting is reinforced.

Joan's parents wished she had been born a boy and they never clarified what else they wanted her to be except that so she "tried to die by being catatonic" (ibid.). Joan had to die, otherwise her feelings would have killed her. She felt that she did not know who on earth she was. "The only thing I was sure of was being a 'catatonic, paranoid schizophrenic'. I had seen that written on my chart. That at least had substance and gave me an identity and personality" (Joan, ibid.). In order to change, she needed to be liked for herself. Then a diagnosis would be redundant. (27)

Laing described the self as simultaneously empty and starving: "The whole orientation of the self is in terms of longing to eat, yet destroying the food or being destroyed by it" (Laing, 1959). Joan describes it in terms of trying to get to the breast but trying to die and also trying not to die. She felt as though she was imprisoned in a bottle, unable to be touched, excluding her self from everything. However, her self was being tortured within this prison by the three-way conflict described above. She feared exploring outside the bottle and the people she would encounter "for they are even heavier than those in here, I think...The people are bigger and would push me back into this cave...but I can never get into that shaft of light that creeps in this cave because the people block my way, by mistake, I think, I hope" (ibid.). There is always a real self, no matter how far it is buried in or accustomed to the cave. Joan could not, ought not or dare not be herself as an embodied person.

"Blow up the cave with dynamite!" (Joan, cited in Laing, 1959) She wanted a doctor to force his way in because she did not feel that she had the strength. (28) She wanted to cry and for her tears not to be wiped away. Perhaps she wanted to physically see her pain. Wiping her tears away would be far too quick and easy a process to do justice to the damage she had experienced.

A doctor must be a rock that never rolls away no matter how much he is pushed. Joan believed that her doctor should fight his way into what she felt, not ask permission or deliberate as this would cause her to feel guilty. She wanted to be 'dead' and 'hidden' and would consequently hate the doctor. However, this hate would be "the only way to get started" (ibid.). The doctor must have firm convictions and be sure that his approach is correct. He must understand the hate enough not to be hurt by it. Doctors often seem frightened of someone who is frightened and so decide to medicate to re-establish control (see 'Medication and Countertransference', Chapter 5).

Joan described how 'schizophrenics' cannot trust anyone and how their fear overrides the desire to break from their safe and familiar cycle. She perceived loving as impossible at the beginning because of the fear of exposing herself as a helpless baby. "The patient can't feel safe until he is absolutely sure the doctor understands what is needed and will provide it" (ibid.).

"Meeting you made me feel like a traveller who's been lost in a land where no-one speaks his language. Worst of all, the traveller doesn't even know where he should be going. He feels completely lost and helpless and alone. Then, suddenly, he meets a stranger who can speak English. Even if the stranger doesn't know the way to go, it feels so much better to be able to share the problem with someone, to have him understand how badly you feel. If you're not alone, you don't feel hopeless anymore. Somehow it gives you life and a willingness to fight again" (Joan, cited in Laing, 1959).

Laing and Esterson met with and interviewed eleven families of females who had been diagnosed with 'schizophrenia'. They viewed 'schizophrenia' as a social process that is comprehensible as a response to family transactions and interactions. They transferred the onus of inadequacy from the 'schizophrenic' to the family.

The Abbotts would exchange nods, winks, gestures and knowing smiles in front of their daughter, Maya. She became paranoid because they denied doing this. Maya thus mistrusted her own mistrust. When she was fourteen and began wondering about sex, they told her that she did not have any thoughts of that nature. If a person's ideas and character are already known, they might assume that speaking is unnecessary. Maya's parents contradicted her memory, feelings, perceptions, motives and intentions. She was eventually diagnosed on the basis that she suffered from catatonia, paranoia, impoverishment of affect, autistic withdrawal, auditory hallucinations and confusion of ego boundaries. It seems plausible that many children would withdraw and become paranoid when raised in such circumstances.

The other girls had similar experiences. Lucie's parents told her that she would be kidnapped, raped or murdered if she went out alone. Her father told her she was a slut, a prostitute and said she should be 'trodden underfoot'. All of Lucie's statements were invalidated. Sarah was bewildered by the double standards of her family because she religiously adhered to what she had been taught. Ruth's illness was defined by her mother as wearing coloured stockings, not going to jazz club, being interested in writers and art, bringing friends home and staying out late. When questioned whether she had to agree with people around her, she replied, "Well if I don't, I usually land up in hospital" (Laing and Esterson, 1964). Mary claimed her mother instructed her to do one thing and then questioned her as to why she did not do the opposite. Her mother put thoughts in her head when she wanted a mind of her own. Agnes' father invalidated each of her activities or interests that might have helped her to establish her autonomy. He defined her illness as being worried, getting on his nerves, going to church, not telling him her thoughts and liking a boy yet being unsure of whether she loved him. Her paranoid ideas included "saying the hospital hadn't helped her" (ibid.). Opinions cannot be incorrect.

All these girls were struggling to make sense of a senseless situation. However, the psychiatrists regarded this as 'schizophrenia'. The parents contradicted and fought their daughters' efforts to achieve independence and autonomy. (29) The eleven daughters thus assumed roles of passivity, dependence, chastity, obedience and docility.

Chadwick (1997), a sufferer and survivor of 'schizophrenia', was conditioned by his mother to loathe and deny the soft, feminine, epicurean, hypersensitive aspect of his character. People are often raised with the idea that to succeed in life, they must play a particular role and gain acceptance for it. If this role deviates from the person's perception of their self or what he/she thinks is right, an emptiness will ensue and the person will attempt to fill that void.

Often negative family relationships are enormously magnified due to parents discouraging the use of people outside the family as sources of information and corrective identification. The compensatory symbiotic cushion of one's family conceals the manifest pathology from the scrutiny and expectations of objective outsiders. Parents are insecure about having their beliefs and values challenged by their children.

Social pressures define the individual's family lifestyle as abnormal yet psychological primitiveness prevents them from surviving in the larger world. In other words, their family relationships are dysfunctional yet they do not possess the skills to enter into society. They thus face an impossible dilemma. Infantilisation and denying one's vulnerabilities ensue. (30) Pathological equilibrium occurs and then social feedback about ineptitude and the loss of pathological family symbiosis, which has compensated for it, triggers 'schizophrenia' and this exacerbates whilst the child deliberates.

Lidz stated that "meanings alter in the service of emotional needs...when all paths to the future seem blocked...one can simply alter his perceptions of his own needs and motivations and those of others; one can abandon causal logic or change the meaning of events; one can regress, retreating to a period in childhood when reality gave way before the wish..." (1973, cited in Robbins, 1992). Therefore regression and 'schizophrenia' appear to be the only options available to such an individual.

Chapter 5

Psychoanalytic Perspectives of 'Schizophrenia'

Psychoanalysis with 'Schizophrenics'

'Schizophrenia's alleged biological underpinnings are now widely considered to remove it from the realm of psychoanalysis entirely. Information on the benefits of psychoanalysis has often been dismissed as anecdotal due to the absence of rigorous research methodology thus causing interest in it to wane. A number of psychoanalytic institutes no longer include the study of 'schizophrenia' in their curriculum and there has been a decrease in the number of psychoanalytic studies of this illness. (31)

Freud viewed 'schizophrenia' as a psychological problem and although he was fascinated by Schreber's psychosis (1911) and attempted to treat some psychotic patients (eg. the 'Wolf Man'), he mostly practised with neurotics. He did not have access to hospitalised 'schizophrenic' patients. Therefore his theoretical formulations are derived from paranoid patients and from Schreber's biography. He believed that patients resist therapy to protect themselves from the discomfort of change. Most psychoanalysts have followed Freud's model apart from Jung, Abraham and Brill who worked in mental hospitals with 'schizophrenics'. E. Bleuler noted that when he applied Freud's psychoanalytic ideas to his patients at Burgholzli, three times as many were discharged.

Freud's theory of libido as a substance or energy, combined with his theory of narcissism as libido turned toward the self, suggested that 'schizophrenics' could not form a transference or close relationships. He thus believed psychoanalysis to be ineffective with 'schizophrenics'. Rosenfeld proposed that it is difficult to recognise and interpret 'schizophrenic' transference-phenomena but that a transference does exist.

Nunberg (1920) observed a 'schizophrenic' patient for a long period of time who related most of his experiences to the transference. Nunberg stated that the transference was mostly on the homosexual anal level yet the paper described object relations on the oral level. The patient lost interest in the analyst as an external object at the height of the oral-sadistic transference yet retained the internal object relation.

Laforgue (1936) conducted analysis successfully with a 'schizophrenic' girl who was so anxious at the beginning of the treatment that she escaped to the waiting room after only a few minutes. By persistent analysis of the negative transference, she gradually talked freely, became less anxious and developed a positive transference.

Conversely, Federn (1943) proposed that 'schizophrenic' patients could only be treated in the positive transference. He discontinued treatment if negative transferences appeared. He did not interpret either positive or negative transference.

Rosen (1946/7, 1950) dealt with both positive and negative transference in 'schizophrenic' patients by reassurance and interpretation. Other Americans, such as Fromm-Reichmann and Harry Stack Sullivan who discarded the concept of libido, stressed the importance of transference in 'schizophrenia' and proposed that an infant is capable of an object relation from its birth.

Sullivan influenced the notion that psychoanalysis could cure 'schizophrenia' during World War II but this has been followed by mutual disillusionment and estrangement. He believed that analysts must use any means at their disposal to reach the 'schizophrenic'. Based on his intuition that 'like can help like' and, perhaps, his own experience with a psychotic episode, he ran a unit for young men with 'schizophrenia' during the 1920's. He staffed the unit with shy, introverted male attendants and observed that providing an experience of reciprocal trust, which he felt many patients had missed during critical development, could be beneficial. Sullivan described 'schizophrenic' psychopathology as the lasting residue of unsatisfactory interpersonal experiences and saw a basic mistrust of others as central to the condition. Patients expected harm from others, demonstrated marked ambivalence in relationships, had difficulty separating personal thoughts and impulses from those of others and showed pervasive passivity.

Torrey (1988) stated that it "is not only negligent, it is malpractice" (cited in Robbins, 1992) to treat 'schizophrenia' with psychoanalytic therapy. Eissler (1951) asserted that 'schizophrenics' respond to almost any sympathetic psychotherapeutic approach due to their acute awareness of the 'primary process' in other people's minds. However, he did not perceive this peculiarity as a transference phenomenon which could be related to a primitive object relationship. This question of transference has divided the psychoanalytic movement.

Searles admitted his problems of countertransference while growing as a psychotherapist with 'schizophrenics' and contributed to the concept of therapeutic symbiosis to understand them. He never claimed to cure all patients but he could move them along the continuum from 'completely crazy' to more normal functioning (in some cases, up to 90% normal). He, like Kleinians, insisted that primitive psychotic processes are at work in all of us all the time, though it is only in severe psychosis that the person is dominated by them. The patient susses out the unconscious processes and vulnerabilities of the therapist. They lead the therapist to experience internal reprojection which exaggerates that aspect of their own true personality (Searles, 1965).

Otto Will stated the problems of affect frequently found in intensive work with 'schizophrenics'. Both Searles and Will have helped stimulate the use of individual intensive psychotherapy with chronic 'schizophrenics'.

Rosenfeld published the Mildred case in 1947 which was considered to be the first case of a 'schizophrenic' being cured by psychoanalysis. Three years later, Lacan's "Ecrits" were published. Lacan did not state whether or not psychoanalysis could cure 'schizophrenia'. He derived his theory of psychosis from his commentary of Freud's study of Schreber's Memoirs. Lacan's understanding of the 'schizophrenic' as having a defective relation to language can explain four characteristics of 'schizophrenic' behaviour: the fragmented body image; the lack of realistic evaluation of the world; so-called bisexuality; and confusion of birth and death (De Waelhens, 1984). Psychoanalysis uses language in its treatment. However, language in 'schizophrenics' is deficient. This can be counteracted if the therapist uses language, first to repair at the imaginary (unconscious) level and then to make an attempt to correct in the symbolic (linguistic dimension, sometimes referred to as the 'Other').

Based on Freud's categories, the diagnostic category for 'schizophrenia', accepted by Lacanian psychoanalysts, is: "Schizophrenia manifests itself through fragmentary delusional formations and hallucinations; incoherence of speech and thought; blunted or bizarre affective responses and catatonic responses, all of which represent the subject's attempts to deal with a collapse of the representation of the body, or inability to construct that representation in relation with the small other [i(o)]'. As a result, the body becomes a place which is almost impossible to inhabit" (Rodríguez, 1999).

The task of the psychoanalyst is to foster a self-reflective attitude in the patient towards his own body signs in order to facilitate their translation into verbal symbols. This translation is a most difficult process, especially for 'schizophrenics' as their language is symbolic in the first place.

Rosine Lefort, a Lacanian, believed the analyst should be particularly passive and act as an object and secretary, yet still actively listen and do silent work. This facilitates the subject's attempts to divide the Other, articulate a demand and extract the object from the Other. If the analyst's approach was more active, the subject's attempts to separate the object from the Other would be frustrated and this may impose passivity upon the patient. In a quiet setting, the patient's desire may emerge. This is the creative side of the transference which is required for the birth of the Other and thus the subject.

Medication and Countertransference

The symbiotic phase, a phase of early development, often features in the relationship between a 'schizophrenic' patient and therapist although it is pathologically extended and often has not been successfully mastered. There is a loss of self-object differentiation demonstrating a diffusion in ego boundaries between patient and therapist. Projection and identification ensue. However the non-psychotic part of the adult patient can participate in the therapeutic relationship and respond to ideas and emotions.

The symbiosis can be comforting or terrifying for both patient and therapist. The therapist should be able to flip between symbiotic relatedness and a more detached, mature, objective analytic approach to allow the patient the freedom of exploring and resolving their fixations and ideas. The therapist, in his analytic capacity, should also interpret the unconscious meanings of the patient's fantasies.

Regression to a childhood state is often far repressed in the unconscious. However, triggers can easily cause the patient to enter into non-verbal, intense and mutually gratifying relationships (eg. mother/baby). It is possible for the 'schizophrenic' to project these distortions onto the therapist and perceive the conflict this causes in the therapist.

Countertransference can thus be an invaluable tool in the relationship between patient and therapist (Winnicott 1949, Little 1957, Heimann 1950). The therapist's unconscious conflicts and reaction to the relationship often give him clues as to the patient's history. However, this can interfere with progress if the therapist does not analyse or express his own feelings and maintain conscious control. Often, ideas and feelings are shared and both parties can become caught up in the confusion of the psychosis. The therapist may harbour murderous and sadistic thoughts towards the patient, illustrating that it is an incorporation of the patient's own hostility and sadism.

"The therapist's use of pharmacological intervention at this time represents an unconscious attempt to firmly localise in the patient both that which has been projected into the therapist by the patient, as well as those conflicts within the therapist accurately perceived and accentuated by the patient" (Levy, 1993). It also illustrates to the patient that their feelings are too unbearable to experience and therefore must be dampened by medication. This reinforces the patient's belief that their feelings are too dangerous to be dealt with. Also, the interpersonal boundaries between therapist and patient become evident once again and can cancel out the value of any previously shared ideas.

Therefore medication might be used to block the patient's growth in a variety of ways. "Medication may represent an abandonment of hope about increased self-understanding through insight, a communication to the patient that his impulses are too dangerous to express without being dampened by drugs, or a warning to the patient that changes he is making are intolerable to the therapist" (Levy, 1993). Thus the patient's belief that he/she has a disease which can only be treated by medication is reinforced. Conversely, drugs may be withheld due to the gratification received by the therapist in experiencing the maximum intensity of the patient's regression.

Casement (1985) believes that many patients who reside in mental hospitals have been in therapy where they could not safely express the intensity of their feelings, i.e. they were not 'held' by the therapist. The therapist must be able to tolerate and survive being genuinely in touch with the patient's feelings. Casement says "the best containment is a good interpretation. That means being able to make sense of what a patient is saying and feeling, and being able to convey this to the patient" (1985). An example of this is described below in the 'Case Material'.

One twenty-eight year-old woman, who had withdrawn from the world because of several cases of sexual abuse by her father, hated everybody apart from her horse. She was unresponsive in therapy and, on one occasion, said that she wished the session would end so she could go to the stables. The therapist was angry and explained that people, rather than horses, have something to offer. He even threatened her that one day she would have to give up her horse. He then decided medication would "help get things moving" (Levy, 1993). Here the therapist felt disgusted, murderous, jealous and ridiculous, the patient having emptied these feelings onto the therapist. He could not bear what he was experiencing and thus recommended medication. He lost the ability to use the projective-incorporative process and could not objectively evaluate the situation. He did not use his feelings to the benefit of the therapy. 'Schizophrenics' are afraid of change and so keep therapists at arm's length. This often causes the therapist to keep the patient at arm's length because they see something of themselves in the patient (Rosberg, 1999).

Therapists can often experience previously repudiated regressive yearnings which their patients, in turn, gratify. Therapists may enjoy the "crazy hours" (Levy, 1993) and regalement spent with their patients as it gives them a rare opportunity to experience ideas and feelings that are discouraged in 'normal' situations. They consequently might feel guilty at this enjoyment and decide to medicate the patient. This is due to wanting to treat their own craziness manifest in their enjoyment of their patient's bizarre and uninhibited mode of relationship. Therefore both patient and therapist are gratified. It is also likely, in some cases, that the therapist is unsure of how to proceed and so, to feel useful, prescribes medication to define who is in distress. However, in a situation such as this, the therapist should realise that his own feelings are his patient's projections and that the patient obtains gratification and pleasure in his bizarre ideas.

The therapist should be enthusiastic, interested, optimistic, perceptive, patient and wise. A growing rapport should be fostered throughout. It can be dull and depressing when the patient mourns the loss of his omnipotent psychotic feelings (post-psychotic depression). The excitement should not be recaptured. Even the therapist might lose protective narcissistic fantasies and often covertly support and encourage bizarre ideas in the patient to prevent the appearance of painful depressed feelings. The patient may wish to be left alone and retreat and the therapist may feel he is intruding on the patient. In such cases, the patient needs more independence.

Case Material

Casement's Teddy was twenty-four when he began therapy. For two years he had been treated at home on Stelazine as a catatonic 'schizophrenic'. He had been in and out of mental hospitals. Teddy had been silent for two years but had started giving one-word answers to questions, usually "Yes" or "No."

Casement began by questioning him to discover something of his past. Although he learned details about Teddy's home and school, no real progress was made. When Casement was silent, this also had no effect on Teddy. Casement imagined what it must be like having social workers constantly firing questions at him. It struck him how persecutory this could be. It was as if Casement were trying to force himself through Teddy's near total exclusion of the outside world. "Teddy's mode of answering seemed to be a compromise between his need to defend himself from intrusion and the pressures for him to speak" (Casement, 1985). Casement needed to be aware of Teddy's need for space and separateness in a world that had become persistently intrusive.

The patient should not always be left to speak first. "There are occasions when we need to recognise that the patient has already started the session with silence. We are less likely to get into a sterile game of waiting if we learn to 'read' a patient's silence, and sometimes to respond tentatively to what we sense as the underlying communication which is being conveyed in this" (Casement, 1990).

Before the next session, Casement rearranged the chairs so they were facing in the same direction. He said, "I have arranged the chairs differently today for a reason that I will try to explain. I have been thinking how it might feel being you here, with a social worker who has been firing all these questions at you. I have also wondered if it might be easier for us both if I didn't sit so directly opposite you – looking as if I am expecting you to look back at me.

When I imagine being in your place, with all those questions coming at me, I feel as if someone were trying to get inside me – forcing me to give away bits of myself that I might not want to give away. I have an image of being surrounded by people trying to force me to talk, and wanting to hide from them. I can also imagine myself not talking to anyone, as a way of trying to build a wall around me to keep people out.

Unfortunately, until today, I have been failing to recognise that you might be needing to keep a wall of silence as a way of keeping me out and at a safe distance" (1985). At this, Teddy turned to face Casement with a look of interest. Teddy began, "It's funny you put it like that. I have often thought of myself as hiding under a man-hole cover, in a drain, with people trying to find me – and sewage down below. I'm not afraid of drains. It's people that smell. They make it difficult for me to breathe. My mother suffocates me. She treats me like a little boy. I am really a man inside, you know. She doesn't realise that" (ibid.).

Casement was astonished at how Teddy opened up, venturing something for the first time in two years. There was still a long way to go but Teddy was able to build upon this. In the second year of therapy, he found himself a job in a toy shop. There he could relate to parents and children on his own terms.

Casement began treating **Miss W.** whilst she was in hospital. She was taking Stelazine and he could not access her. She seemed wooden and lifeless as if she were trying to speak through cotton wool. When discharged from hospital, Miss W. admitted that she had found it difficult to make use of Casement's visits because she felt "so far removed from other people" and "fuzzed up with pills" (Casement,1985).

After two years of therapy, Miss W.'s mother died. She became psychotic and was hospitalised again. When Casement saw her she said, "Yoga... Falling... Everything falling... No stopping... Being held... In pieces... Six months since... Hadn't been since... I'm falling again... I can't stop falling" (ibid.).

Casement realised that Miss W. was referring to her first visit to yoga since her mother had died and that her references to 'falling' were possibly related to Winnicott's definition of 'falling for ever' as one of the 'unthinkable anxieties' and 'going to pieces' as another (Casement, 1985). She had returned to a regressed state in which she became the child who had nobody to hold her. Casement replied, "When you were last at the Yoga class your mother was still alive. You may have been able to delay taking in the fact of her death until you returned to this class. On going back, I think you suddenly realised how your world had changed since your last time there. The person who once held you as a child is no longer there for you now. Your familiar world, in which there always used to be a mother for you, now feels broken into pieces. This has left you feeling that you are falling, with no-one to stop the falling, and no-one to hold you together" (ibid.).

Miss W. responded, "The falling has stopped now...You are holding me together...You have stopped the falling" (ibid.).

During the space of half an hour, Miss W. went from hallucinating psychosis to being able to remain in touch with reality. Casement's interpretation 'held' her. He was in touch with her feelings and so she did not feel so alone. Her unmanageable experience became manageable. Therefore she did not need to return to psychosis to avoid the unbearable pain of becoming suddenly aware of being motherless.

Later in the treatment, Casement was to take a summer break and told Miss W. that he felt she would be alright whilst he was away. Then, the session before his holiday, Miss W. arrived in an agitated state and was on the edge of psychosis. She said that she had been feeling steady at home and at work but had begun to "feel wobbly" on her way to the session. Casement recalled her last session and listened to himself reassuring Miss W. This was not helpful to her. Reassurance never reassures! He was not in touch with her precarious state, not being as anxious as she was. He was actually unconsciously communicating to her his denied anxiety about her capacity to cope on her own. He possibly did not want to hear that she was anxious about coping without him. Sometimes a therapist acts to satisfy his own feelings instead of hearing what he least wants to hear.

After realising this, Casement interpreted, "I believe I was unhelpful to you in your last session. I may have put some of my own anxiety into you about whether you would cope during the summer break. When I was trying to be reassuring about this, I think it probably had the opposite effect on you as if I had been trying to brush aside what you were feeling. I know I can only really help you when I am letting myself remain in touch with what you are feeling, rather than suggesting you could be feeling some other way" (ibid.).

Miss W. replied, "I am glad you have realised that. I felt you were rather going on about how I would cope and I wasn't at all sure I could. Then you seemed to be far away from me. It made me feel all alone again. Now I don't feel so alone" (ibid.). She then returned from the edge of psychosis.

Casement had to contain Miss W. by remaining in touch with her. Stelazine had contained her medically but she could not be reached emotionally or feel held by insight or a relationship. A therapist must be able to survive being tested to the "bottom of the trough" and out again. "This new experience can begin to expunge the deep impression of past experience...With some damaged patients we take on a terrible responsibility. We could make things worse for them if we fail to survive at the point when they most need to test our capacity for survival. So we should only offer containment in a relationship, as an alternative to medication or to hospital containment, with a full awareness of the risks that may be involved. We must know what we could be taking on" (Casement, 1985).

Susan

Susan began treatment with Marion Milner in November, 1943 after she had been removed from a mental hospital by an English couple. There was a major debate at the time between the Kleinians and the proponents of ego psychology about whether psychoanalysis could cure 'schizophrenia'. Milner had been influenced by Klein and Winnicott and believed transference to be an effective tool in curing 'schizophrenia'. However, she theorised that psychoanalysis alone could not cure it which contradicted Klein's view.

Soler proposed that Milner did not cure a 'schizophrenic'. The disappearance of Milner's own anxiety was her perception of the cure. (32) Also, there was no mention of hallucinations, impaired speech, dissociation or language dysfunction. However, Susan did hear continuous music in her head to drown out the frightening noise of her parents arguing. This resulted in her creating a prison that she could not escape from. (33)

Susan grew up with an alcoholic step-father who once tried to sexually abuse her when she was in his bed. Her mother wished Susan had been a boy and alternated between blaming her for everything and making a fuss of her. (34) She would not let Susan or her sister walk before the age of two for fear of them becoming bow-legged and used to call Susan greedy when she asked for extra food. She would often attempt to frighten Susan and sometimes would not speak for days, frequently wandering off saying she was never returning. Consequently, Susan could not bear to be separated from her mother. (35)

Susan was very musical and longed for piano lessons but her mother let Susan's unmusical sister take them instead. Susan was taken to ballet classes at nine years old but was not allowed to practise at home because of lack of space. She would not practise in the park because of the embarrassment of being seen so she practised in her head. She spoke of how she came to "live in her body." This is very significant and illustrates how paranoia is engendered when one has to turn inward.

At school nobody played with her and her sister would not talk to her. An old male neighbour whom she regularly visited gave her candy and toys in return for masturbating against her. Perhaps she was attempting to master the situation through her repeated visiting of him. When Susan attempted to disclose this to her mother, her mother replied, "Don't tell me - it will kill me." Susan developed rituals at the age of ten such as swimming across the tidal mouth of the river and picking up all the pins she saw.

A friend's mother, Mrs Dick, tried to educate Susan because her mother had failed to do so but was convinced that she had designs on her husband. Mrs Dick eventually died of a cardiac arrest and it was this event that triggered Susan's heart pains and vomiting. Susan was admitted into hospital six weeks after Mrs Dick's death for functional nervous diseases. When her mother visited her, several people commented that they could not tell whether it was Susan or her mother that was the patient. Her mother seemed to have no recognition of Susan's separate existence. (36) She also made sexual overtures to a love interest of Susan's. Susan eventually married.

Whilst in hospital, Susan was assigned to a male psychiatrist. On their first meeting, she mentioned jumping out of a window to him. He replied that talking like that would land her in a proper mental hospital. He also told her that she had nothing to feel guilty about which stopped her exploring her problems.

Susan's therapy with Milner was facilitated by her drawings. Drawing does not offer the resistance of articulated sentences and gives free rein to the imagination. Drawing was also Susan's way of creating a bridge between herself and Milner and a basis for communication. Milner viewed Susan's drawings as her private language that anyone would have to learn how to read and speak if they were to help her. Her drawings were symbols showing emotion that she could not show on her face. She internalised all her pain and so did not outwardly react to anyone or anything apart from blushing (which she later said was a replacement for being hurt). In other words, the world was not really outside her. If she accepted that Milner was actually outside her, she would be flooded with intense grief, pain, anger and desolation that would be beyond endurance and drive her either to suicide or attempted murder of Milner.

Milner's acceptance of Susan and her drawings had the effect of modifying her prohibitive inner mother image. When drawing, the paper became a substitute for the responsive ideal mother, receiving the movements of her hand and returning it to her eyes. In other words, it fostered a reciprocal give-and-take interchange on a primitive non-verbal level. In fact, it replicated a relation to an ideal mother, Milner, who would be with her whenever she needed.

Susan was often inaccessible to any comment or suggestion from Milner. Milner compared this scenario to an infant who cannot suck any more from the breast until it receives a gentle pat on the back from the mother which usually leads to a belch. In other words, Susan could not deal with new material until she had addressed her current issues. All her concentration was directed at her remorse at having ECT. She identified analysis with the shock treatment and this inhibited the development of the transference to Milner. (37) She viewed any improvement from the analysis as a condoning of the ECT. Milner interpreted that Susan felt all the good in her would be destroyed if she displayed it. She always snubbed compliments.

When Susan obsessively spoke of people in her present environment, Milner tried to impress upon her that they represented split-off and projected bits of herself. She dreamt of a baby, perhaps representing herself, that could not be born and of an impulse to kill babies. "Certainly the urge to kill a child seemed to occur most often when she was nearest to becoming conscious of her dependence on me, with all the wishes and needs of infancy; that is, nearest to becoming born into the real world of her own body, for this would bring all the bad memories of the utter terrors and rages that dependence had brought in her actual infancy" (ibid.). Susan and her mother were bound together - therefore blocked against being born. The terrifying internal mother image had to be disposed of before it would be safe to be re-born.

Milner believed that Susan wanted to outwardly attack somebody so she could see something tangible to feel guilty about. She disclosed a wish to kill her mother. Her rational self-conscious ego had to be torn to pieces if she was ever to achieve a re-birth. Milner believed that Susan had to realise that it was safe to go to pieces in order to come together in a new way but that she was terrified of coming together again.

Susan thought Milner was making her own forbidden wishes emerge from repression and thus that Milner was the devil. An interplay was required to produce a new kind of togetherness or a unity of subject and object. She suffered a girl's deepest anxiety, comparable to a boy's castration fear, that the inside of her body would be destroyed by a vengeful enemy mother in revenge for her own wishes to get inside her mother and attain everything she imagined to be there for herself. She was terrified of destroying, being unable to protect either the good inner image or its external representative from her own destructiveness. Milner perceived the devil that possessed Susan as a personification of this kind of defence against experiencing the pain and grief at loss of what was loved. When she cried, "Give me back my feelings!" (ibid.) perhaps she was showing the intense battle between the devil and the human part in her. She doubted which was strongest: her love or hate.

When Susan felt hate, she felt the whole landscape shimmered with her hate. Perhaps her bodily excitement exceeded the bounds of her body, escaped through her eyes and animated the surrounding world. This could have been due to the state of continual fear in which she had lived her childhood. It had caused a shrinking or contracting of her whole body and consciousness (like a spider drawing in its legs and shamming dead) so that there was no space in which feelings of bodily excitement could be contained. "The tightly held narrowing of awareness is incapable of encompassing and holding states of feeling, thus they are pent up, have no room to expand within the body and consequently may burst out in explosive action" (ibid.).

Susan had a day-dream of a river with logs floating down it. On one bank there was a danger of scalping and on the other, emptiness. Milner interpreted this as a dilemma of whether to face the real world with all the dread of violence, of attacking, living through memories or turning inwards where there seemed to be total emptiness. The sawn-off logs could represent both her own cut-off spontaneous impulses and the wish to bite off a bit of Milner.

Susan spoke of her obsessions and of being terrified of reaching the centre (nucleus) of the circle inside her. If she penetrated the inside of the circle, she and fear would be one. Milner viewed the circle as her anus: she would be able to feel herself expelling. Susan perhaps perceived Milner and her mother as her own faecal possessions that were out of her body and dead (murdered). (38) Milner also interpreted the inner circle as either her mouth containing her mother's breast, when she had drawn a dot inside the circle, or her empty mouth when the circle was hollow. Therefore penetrating the circle would represent identifying with the nipple and it being bitten off when withdrawn from her.

Susan once dreamt that she was lying face down on top of all the mess in her old home and calling her mother mad, perhaps signifying that she was trying to put order into the chaos and mess that was her mother's madness. However, she must have had memories of the good mother in order to survive and these eventually fused together with her experience of Milner's care to make an internal mother that fed her, contained her and showed many sides to her character. She began to accept being bitten into.

Susan drew a picture of two figures actively managing the sails of a boat with no rudder. Milner interpreted this as Susan and herself in the analysis (boat), delving into the unconscious (sea/keel) but being unsure of the direction (no rudder). There was a theme of the number four in her drawings perhaps representing herself, her unconscious, Milner and Milner's unconscious.

She eventually began to articulate her impulses instead of acting: "I want to hit your breasts with my fists." She also dreamt that she knifed her best friend in the stomach and felt upset. This was a great improvement because she had always kept actions and results separate. Milner believed this more undifferentiated phase of mental functioning to have emerged through her development of the symbol of water in her drawings. (39)

Susan finally realised that if thoughts could cause things to go wrong, they could put things right. She often laughed at herself when relishing the incongruity between what would be sensible behaviour and how she felt she had behaved. She was able to do this through listening to herself. She had to release the need that destroyed what it loved. (40)

There were definite positive signs pointing to her recovery. She reported that she felt marvellous for ten minutes whilst having a music lesson. She also spoke of a holiday abroad where she had suddenly "let fly" and a young man had commented on how beautiful she looked. She did not feel as if she wanted to die when awakening in the morning. There were also episodes where she related incidents pertaining to her childhood. She spoke of demoralising her cat and hitting it for being greedy but the cat did not understand why (the cat being a psychical representation of herself). She blamed herself for her cat's greediness and was afraid that she would kill the cat.

Susan said, "The shock of the realisation that one could have been unconscious for so long a time seems almost to send one into unconsciousness again...Being unaware of oneself and consequently of other people makes it impossible to observe and question one's own actions so one behaves as one will, with no consideration for anything or anybody" (ibid.).

She eventually had a dream that the old man she used to visit was masturbating his penis but that he did not want her to do anything. She felt so relieved.

Susan visited her mother and comforted her when she was dying in hospital but her mother never thanked her or responded. (41)

When Susan lived by herself, her condition worsened and a doctor informed her that he did not think she would improve. Shortly after this, she requested admittance to a psychiatric hospital. However, she was eventually put into a hostel and began working again. She was still terrified of being violent, throwing herself under a train (42) and merging with a mother who was mad. Her husband was of great comfort and held her in his arms for long periods. She then felt able to take the risks of bringing the most primitive fantasies involving her mouth directly into the transference relation to Milner. However, she gradually weaned herself off her sessions with Milner in 1963.

Milner discovered the necessary role of silence in treating Susan. Making psychological interpretations about transference produced no reaction in Susan. "Slowly, I found I had to give up trying so hard to provide her with explanations, a giving up which I found difficult since she was always clamouring for them. Instead I felt I had to learn to wait and watch and let her know that I was there, watching, and not let myself be seduced into this working too hard for her, trying to tell her, putting into words for her unconscious preoccupations because I came to suspect, if I let myself be seduced, which I constantly did, it could only put off for the moment, perhaps disastrously, her finding what she herself had arrived at" (ibid.).

In desiring Milner to give her interpretations, Susan was cutting herself off from her inner creative source of repair and growth. Susan needed Milner's help in allowing perplexity and in learning to tolerate muddle. Only then could new ideas emerge. If one stops thinking and simply watches, the energy that had previously been invested in thinking is directed back into one's body - "like a crop of vegetation that is ploughed back onto the soil to fertilize it" (ibid.).

Milner also admitted to feeling "battered by her (Susan's) attacks, rueful at how long the analysis had taken and resigned (sometimes) to the gaps in my knowledge that had made me not know how to help her more" (ibid.).

When Susan was back in the 'outside world', she was continually preoccupied with hiding her illness. Milner believed that one reason for the extreme length of her analysis was that it took so long to find a place for her to live, other than a hospital, where the fact of her illness was both known and tolerated by those around her. Susan did attend a therapeutic group which benefitted her enormously.

Rosenfeld's (1952) patient was a male in his twenties who suffered from hallucinations, was confused and sometimes violent. He was said to be dangerously impulsive, withdrawn and occasionally mute. Neither doctors nor nurses could make contact with him yet he showed interest in Rosenfeld and the analytical procedure from the start. From the first session there were signs of a positive transference but by the third session, a violent negative transference had emerged. Rosenfeld constantly related his own interpretations of the patient's words and behaviour back to him and attempted to relate the analytical material to the transference situation. Although Rosenfeld sometimes had very little material on which to base his interpretations, the patient often displayed relief or anxiety in the face of these interpretations, confirming them directly or indirectly and sometimes even correcting them. Rosenfeld never used direct reassurance.

In the first session, the patient said, "Resurrection" and asked Rosenfeld if he was Jesus. Rosenfeld replied that Jesus could perform miracles and that the patient hoped that he would miraculously be able to heal him. This demonstrated that he perceived Rosenfeld as an omnipotent figure. The patient also mentioned his previous doctor and said, "The Russians were our allies" to which Rosenfeld replied that this doctor had been an ally but had now turned against the patient. He was afraid that Rosenfeld would also turn from an ally into an enemy. The patient then said, "This is true" and subsequently became more rational and talkative about his ideas and his past.

He spoke of a boy, his friend, at school and of another boy who sat on the other side of his friend and caused trouble. Rosenfeld stated that the patient liked him (Rosenfeld) but wanted him to himself yet realised he had other friends and patients. He then mumbled that he must have a saw. This implied his inability to separate parts of himself from Rosenfeld. It seems that the patient immediately related his previous experiences to Rosenfeld in the present. His interest in Rosenfeld as an object was unmistakable.

At the second meeting the patient was preoccupied with hallucinations and was out of touch with Rosenfeld. He eventually said, "One has to find one's own roots...I do not know whether it is right liking you too much." Rosenfeld interpreted that he was afraid and that by liking Rosenfeld too much, he would get inside him and consequently lose his own roots and himself. The patient retorted, "I want to go on peacefully in my own way." He then remained still and silent for ten minutes and admitted he was afraid to move. He also stated that he had a heavy burden on his shoulder. Perhaps, through introjection, (43) Rosenfeld had become an inner burden to him.

In the next session the patient constantly laughed (44), was very restless and made sweeping movements with his hands as if he was brushing Rosenfeld aside. He then stated, increasing his aggressive laughter, "No good at all..." Rosenfeld viewed his reaction as frustration that a miraculous, quick cure had not taken place and he felt that through his anger and disappointment, he had destroyed Rosenfeld and the treatment. He subsequently became frightened and then pointed to Rosenfeld's blue diary saying it was brown. The patient thought his anger had changed Rosenfeld into faeces and that, by means of revenge, Rosenfeld was putting the faeces back into him. Violent negative transference was evident in this session.

He later illustrated that the burden on his shoulders represented all the problems inside him, his introjected objects, anxieties, depressions, persecutions and his own bad self. When he expelled his burden he seemed to distribute it to innumerable people and consequently felt split into many men who were all regarded as persecutors, including Rosenfeld. He then complained of losing parts of himself. The patient also withdrew interest. In fact, his withdrawal from the external world was related to his fear of persecution. When the external object representing the world had been attacked, the world was not only felt to be destroyed but also the external world and the objects representing it became persecutors. Thus the withdrawal was used as a defence against external persecutors. (45) It therefore seemed that the patient could understand and respond to the interpretations of his persecutory fears in the transference situation. He looked as if he was much less troubled by hallucinations at the end of the session and had ceased laughing.

In the fourth session he said, "That happened before...that was the last time." This perhaps illustrated his fear that Rosenfeld would leave him as his previous doctor had, by way of retaliation, due to his attempts to undermine the analysis in the previous session. The patient accepted this interpretation and said, "I want to do everything to help." The patient continually worked through his negative transference by repeating and then being fearful of repeating earlier experiences.

In the fifth session the patient demonstrated how confused he was that his father had left him to be treated in England and had returned to their home abroad. He then said, "Atheism" which Rosenfeld interpreted as a disbelief in anybody because of his father's departure at various stages in his life. He also, through stating that his previous doctor had committed suicide, referred to his own suicidal feelings when the psychiatric sessions ceased.

He then began to look friendly and confidently at Rosenfeld as if he wanted to explain everything to him. He said, "If one goes all the way one cannot retake everything," signifying that if he loved or believed in somebody, he wanted to go all the way or enter that person. He would thus be mixed up, confused and frequently unable to withdraw himself. (46) Also if that person (Rosenfeld) left the patient, he would lose himself (as well as

Rosenfeld). The patient agreed wholeheartedly with this interpretation. He then uttered, "A big-boned man eats a lot." Rosenfeld construed that the patient was warning him of his greed and desire to eat him up.

The patient demonstrated that it was oral feelings which predominated in his impulses to enter an object - his going 'all the way'. However, when the states of confusion and splitting were more severe, the patient was unable to speak and other ego-functions like co-ordination of movements were disturbed.

It is clear from these case histories that when the patient felt their needs had been recognised and appropriately responded to by the analyst, improvement occurred. "Even though treatment may intermittently look totally hopeless, and the analyst may be made to feel entirely hopeless too, it is most important not to lose sight of the fact that such problems in treatment are often (in themselves) an expression of the patient's unconscious search for some help – never previously found – with serious emotional difficulties" (Casement, 1990).

Chapter 6

The Way Forward

Confrontation Therapy

According to Dr. Jack Rosberg, some traditional psychotherapies have not been effective in treating 'schizophrenics' because their approach has focused on the patient gaining insight and dealing with intrapsychic conflicts. Sometimes these patients cannot process insights well enough to effect behavioural changes. Many patients are not altered by insights because the illness serves as a survival system and he/she fights against change. The patient's perceptions are distorted and they reinforce the internalisation of world destruction fantasies. "These annihilation fantasies frequently produce an unremitting terror which makes the patient's life a never-ending hell" (Rosberg, 1999).

An individual may not be open to treatment in the first few sessions because a relationship has not been formed with the therapist. At some level, every patient wants to tell someone what their life has been like. However, the patient may be too preoccupied with protecting themselves to recognise that help is available. The patient must be persuaded to accept the therapist into their life as their permission may never be given. They have lost so much faith in the world that they cannot afford to place their trust in anyone yet they desperately need someone in their life who genuinely cares about them.

Consider an elevator ride with a stranger. Any potential relationship with that person remains dormant unless one person imposes in some way, eg. by asking the time. While the seeds of relatedness will begin to stir, they will not take root. The interaction requires nothing more than a casual and impersonal reply. However, if the elevator broke down between floors, a relationship centred on the shared history could develop.

"Therapist and patient often ride silently from floor to floor, only dimly aware of one another, each hoping to be ignored until the other reaches his floor and walks out of the door. Casual thoughts might be shared, perhaps even with some purpose beyond an impersonal exchange of information. But what if they do not understand each other? What if one becomes upset? What if one attacks the other? How will they react? Who will try to deal with it? If both therapist and patient simply get off the elevator and ignore their mutual journey, the history they created will have gone for naught" (Rosberg, 1999).

Rosberg invented the psychotherapeutic method of 'Direct Confrontation'. 'Direct Confrontation' is designed to intrude on the patient's sick behaviour, disrupt the psychosis and produce different sets of behaviour that are more consistent with the expectations and demands of society. The psychotherapist must sometimes use words to shock the patient to alert him/her to the fact that he is different to any previous therapist. (47) The patient will have seen many therapists/psychiatrists before and will feel like a failure as he/she is still suffering and will be frustrated because his/her needs have been denied. The patient will be accustomed to a programme of inactivity, passivity and staff apathy.

'Direct Confrontation' focuses on the present dysfunctional behaviour of the patient. An emphasis on problem-solving and reality-based goals can lead to achievements that are ego-building, thus reducing delusional conflicts, reinforcing the patient's tolerance to stress and effecting a sense of relief, freedom and reward. Building on the positive and healthy parts of the patient aids in re-motivating him/her to look towards reality, rather than wallowing in the defences that the psychosis has persuaded him/her to build: for example, violence, threats, withdrawal, autism, catatonia, confused language and logic. The therapist need not attempt to decipher their language. He must be proactive, not reactive, and identify solvable problems, set goals, design interventions to achieve these goals, examine the responses he receives to correct his approach, assess the outcome and efficacy of his strategy and, above all, maintain hope.

Another important treatment issue is to make the patient aware of any behaviours that lead to disrupting regressive reactions and to show how these behaviours affect others. The patient must become responsible for their behaviour and must learn to control their impulses.

If the therapist follows these guidelines, he is telling the patient that he is stronger than the overwhelming aspects of the 'schizophrenia'. There is a sense of safety and security in this for the patient. The therapist should not be afraid of the patient's fear. It is important to continue the confrontation as long as the patient distorts their perception of the therapist's meaning and as long as they manipulate the therapist in an attempt to perpetuate their condition.

The therapist must be established as the dominant force in the patient's life. Anger on the part of the therapist should be viewed as a natural response rather than countertransference. (48) The patient has a need to be stimulated by the therapist's own strong feelings, like a child needs his parents to stimulate, encourage and provide structure. Aggression is fought with aggression. Fire is fought with fire. The therapist must not wait for the patient's approval of the interventions or yield to their inevitable defensive manoeuvres. He must place demands on the patient so they recognise that there is a new energy in their life that must be dealt with. The emotion of the therapist becomes the fuel to ignite the patient into action.

Rosberg has treated patients who have spit at him, wrestled with him, put their fists and their head through walls, etc. He saw these as deliberate ploys to frighten him into not pursuing his treatment, thus leaving the patients' defences in tact. Perhaps, they were tests to ascertain his strength. The patients may have been seeking power in another human being who could offer protection from their life-threatening world.

Contacting the individual is imperative in the first instance. Even the most regressed person is able to be contacted. The patient's ability to make eye contact is a key indicator of probable success. The therapist must stimulate the curiosity of the patient so that he/she becomes sufficiently intrigued to pursue the relationship. Rarely, if ever, do patients successfully ignore and deny the intrusion of the therapist. In fact, quite the converse is true. "The patient acknowledges the therapist by engaging in a wonderful variety of defensive manoeuvres designed to drive the therapist away" (Rosberg, 1990).

The treatment must begin with the rapid disruption of the patient's defensive patterns. The therapist can therefore demonstrate that he is stronger than the patient's delusional system and can contain the patient's terrors. This allows the patient to feel safe, emerge from their 'psychotic world' and establish a relationship with another human for the first time in many years. If the therapist can understand the patient's defensive patterns, he can help them to reconstruct the meaning of their pathogenic experiences and then recovery becomes a possibility. He might say, "There are going to be some changes made today."

The patient must openly acknowledge and confirm that he/she feels safe. If the patient cannot do this, the therapist must insist that the patient shares any concerns about safety. This process introduces the concept that trust can be established and maintained on a verbal level and that words exchanged between two people can symbolise mutual obligations and responsibilities in the context of the relationship.

The therapist can learn more about the subjective world of the patient by surprising them with the unexpected. It can startle the patient into a reaction that acknowledges the presence of the therapist and then the therapist may, in turn, respond. This may disturb the patient's psychological stability and the therapist must be prepared to deal with the patient's intense feelings, eg. terror. The therapeutic assault will increase and the patient may attempt to build more resistances. Symptoms act defensively when the sick organism is attacked. At this time the therapist must not allow any rupture in the alliance to remain unrepaired. The daily sessions may be extraordinarily active with no pauses for relief. If the therapist can maintain this level of persistence and intensity, the patient's defences will weaken and then the therapist's energy, strength and hope will be renewed.

Good behaviour and qualities: for example, the patient's strength, talents, intelligence, sensitivity to others and positive assets (which can remain uncontaminated by the psychosis) are generously rewarded and bad behaviour is rigorously suppressed. This causes the patient to realise that he/she can inspire people by behaving well rather than frightening them. The therapist makes it clear that he cares too much for the patient to allow them to behave like an animal. The patient must never be insulted or violated. Anger must only be expressed at the delusions to demonstrate that delusional assault will not be tolerated. The therapist can be angry at the illness yet convey feelings of concern for the patient. He must remain a powerful and benevolent force in the patient's life.

When the patient behaves inappropriately, the therapist should constantly question the patient, "Why did you say that? Why did you do that?" to suggest to the patient that they are making a choice. The patient must be forced to choose between staying sick and recovering. Making decisions enhances the patient's self-esteem. When the patient is encouraged to acknowledge dysfunctional behaviour, their concept of self is developed and further therapeutic change is possible. The therapist might also reassure the patient by saying, "I am here. I am not going to let your delusions hurt you while we are together. I believe in you and I will not go away until you stop acting crazy. I will not abandon you."

The therapist could try to 'hold' the patient by saying, "You're making me feel frustrated by behaving in this way. Some people might be frightened of you. Maybe you're showing me that you have been frightened. You act like this to protect yourself from anyone who is trying to force their way into your life. You're frightened that if you let me in, you will have to face the pain of the past. You're testing me to see if I am strong enough to withstand your attacks. I *am* strong enough and I am strong enough to feel your pain."

Every morning, the therapist could say, "You are a real person. You have feelings, you have emotions, you have a soul, you have a body and a spirit. You need not be frightened anymore. You will never be alone again. We are a team. You are the most important part of the team. Each day we are going forward together" (Pam Duncan, 2001).

The patient may refuse to talk. This could be due to fear of their psychosis or fear of saying the wrong thing which could either be used against them or to harm the therapist. When the patient is unresponsive, the therapist could attempt to distract them or approach their other senses by picking fragrant flowers from the garden and smelling them, using aromatherapy oils, listening to music, playing with cats and dogs, partaking in aerobics classes, watching comedy programmes on TV, etc.

After the patient begins to talk, the tension in the relationship should be increased by raising the issue of the patient's desire to recover. Does the patient truly want help? What type of help does he/she want? Is he/she willing to make contact with the therapist to meet specific objectives?

When a patient has been reached and begins to disclose information, their behaviour might deteriorate for fear of losing their defences. At this time, the therapist is advised to effect closure. He might say, "Talking coherently might make you frightened. Don't worry about getting sick again. I have no expectations of you. I will keep you safe. The choice is yours" (Rosberg, 1999). Then the therapist might focus the patient on his (the therapist's) own discomfort and confusion, making the patient aware that their speech has had power over the therapist. Thus the patient could exert control over the therapist at this time. In Rosberg's experience, at this stage, the patient rarely, if ever, takes this opportunity. The patient begins to risk being understood by the therapist.

Once the patient's symptoms have diminished, it is the therapist's task to make a greater effort to fill the ensuing emptiness in the patient. Here, concentration on their good qualities must be intensified. The rewards of treatment are very slow in presenting themselves and are often difficult to perceive. It is easy for therapists to yield and retreat at the crucial stage of treatment because of the emotional and physical energy it demands.

"Nobody likes to look inside and see their own pathology mirrored by the patient's psychosis. Nobody likes to experience the feelings of failure and fatigue as the patient appears to win battle after battle. And, most importantly, nobody wants to expose the incompetence they feel when they are asked to take on the well-rehearsed illness of the veteran 'schizophrenic'" (Rosberg, 1999).

Pam Duncan, a confrontation therapist, said that the academic tools she uses are "good common sense, a long fuse, compassion coupled with a deep respect for the humanity of the sufferers of this complex illness, an understanding of the illness and a huge belief in what I am doing" (1999).

The therapist's approach should constantly change with the changing needs of the patient. This process is unconscious and instinctive. "Discard your memory; discard the future tense of your desire; forget them both, both what you knew and what you want, to leave space for a new idea" (Bion, 1980).

Examples of Confrontation Therapy

One 'schizophrenic' patient, at the first meeting, leaned forward in a menacing way and sarcastically asked Rosberg, "What do you want?" in an attempt to push him away. Rosberg lashed back with verbal aggression of his own which startled the patient into reality. This was the beginning of an unusual kind of relationship and the session now proceeded on a different basis. Distancing the patient from the psychosis was critical if a therapeutic alliance was to be formed. Rosberg made an effort to separate himself from those professionals the patient was convinced were conspiring against him. The patient was now certain that Rosberg had the strength to ask him questions and receive answers. Rosberg continued, "I intend to help you to lose your fears. Nobody is going to hurt you. I'll take care of you and protect you. I know the reasons for your fear. I am not going to add to them but I want you to look at me." The patient then replied, "OK, now what do you want to talk about?" The patient actually answered his own question and related his emotional pain. He broke down, began to cry and revealed more of his fears. Rosberg continued to ask the patient to look at him and made an effort to focus the patient on the present (Rosberg, 1999).

Another patient, **Stephanie**, responded viciously and sadistically to Rosberg after he had introduced himself and informed her that he was going to help her. He said, "You've rejected me and I don't like that. It's not fair. It's not human. It's disrespectful and rude." Stephanie replied, "Kill me, spit on me, hit me, cut my head off, pull my hair out." These were all the things she would have tried to do to Rosberg had she not been restrained. Rosberg was tempted "to be violent in return but reason told me this was exactly what she wanted me to do in order that she could perpetuate her condition. As a child, her rage had resulted in cruelty at the hands of her father and she had come to believe that therapists would respond to her rage with sympathy and understanding because they could not allow themselves the reality of *their* own anger. When I realised this, I told her repeatedly and forcefully that I was not her father. I added that although I would not treat her cruelly or revengefully as her father had, I would do whatever I could to make her realise that her acting out would not drive me away but would make me even more insistent that she treat me with respect" (ibid.).

Here, Stephanie perhaps decided to interact with Rosberg until she discovered enough of his weaknesses to destroy him or drive him away, learning all the while how to improve her preparation the next time the threat appeared. She screamed, cried, banged her head on her bed and spat on Rosberg until he was drenched. Rosberg did not feel rejected. Instead, he felt outraged at the arrogance of a psychosis that could remove all humanity from a human being. He was furious that such a bright, creative person was being controlled by murderous impulses. He shouted that she was a dictator and a miserable beast. He continued to ask her why she was so crazy and why she wouldn't let him help her. He would not be driven away. She began to shout, "Kill me. Kill me. Do it today." She may have felt like dying instead of trying to protect herself from her own fears of annihilation. She could not afford to believe that Rosberg would not violate her in response to her own attacks. "To maintain the integrity of her psychosis, it was vital that she do to me as her father had done to her and as she had done to all the others who had tried to help her. She knew, from long experience, that if she could get me to violate her, then she would defeat me" (Rosberg, 1999).

Rosberg yelled at her, "You crazy woman. You don't have to be this way. Who the hell do you think you are, God? How dare you do all these things to people? You think you have the whole world at your side but you are not going to control my life!" At this she continued to spit and kick; Rosberg, all the time saying, "No" repeatedly. He remained close to her but did not touch her and continued to explain that she could not drive him away.

He eventually gained therapeutic access to her. She began to yield to his demands in the hope that he'd go away. The necessity of compromise had been forced upon her and she had to accommodate another human being. Stephanie was not allowed to escape into her primary process. She was forced to deal with the reality of the connection between language and appropriate emotions. This insertion of realistic values and beliefs made Stephanie feel more safe and, at the same time, Rosberg took on more of the burdens of her psychosis. He was prepared to continue waging a battle on Stephanie's behalf which would help her recover.

Anne Sippi was twenty-three when she began treatment with Rosberg. She had suffered from 'schizophrenia' for nine years and was violent 70% of the time. She had been described to Rosberg as a 'nuclear schizophrenic' who was retarded. Rosberg approached her, pulled her hair down and said, "Young Lady, I understand you bite people, you hit people, you kick people and you tear their hair out. That's fine with me because that's exactly what I do." She suddenly noticed his presence. Rosberg was determined not to let her persuade him to leave her alone. He chased her all over the hospital screaming at her. He shouted, "stop being crazy." Three weeks later, she was controlling her impulses more effectively.

Rosberg eventually raised enough money to buy a residential treatment centre in 1978 and named it, 'The Anne Sippi Clinic' (which is still in existence). He employs psychotherapists, a psychiatrist and case managers. The case managers are entrusted with resocialisation and rehabilitation procedures and are under the supervision of each patient's psychotherapist. These procedures are different for each patient because not all can tolerate the same amount of pressure. The managers want to learn and work hard, they have respect and hope for the patients, they are sensitive, they have common sense and they can cope with pressure. Each therapist must spend time outside of their office walking around the unit and talking to every patient. It is difficult to understand a patient's behaviour in an office (a context far removed from the patient's world).

Rosberg also supervises and directs the 'Association for the Psychotherapy of Schizophrenia' (APS). It educates and provides training for professionals and students and helps them develop an understanding of the logic, language and meaning of 'schizophrenia', and develops treatments which provide a more efficacious alternative to a chemical masking of symptoms. In several countries, Rosberg has trained a small cadre of staff who have applied his methods in their hospitals. A sense of hope and promise was revived. He is prepared to offer this service anywhere in the world.

Hearing Voices

Four percent of the population hear voices. Three percent of these have not received a diagnosis of 'schizophrenia'. It is possible that this three percent have sought help from the Hearing Voices Network rather than the medical profession. Many people refuse to listen to and explore their voices. They equate them with insanity and thus psychosis develops. If one's voices are dismissed, bewilderment will ensue.

GroupWork

'Hearing voices' groups have now been established. Group therapy provides a haven where abnormal behaviours are acknowledged, validated, normalised, understood and de-stigmatised. One can move away from isolation and the role of the victim. "I think that when people get together and share ideas, they can achieve amazing things...I've learnt more from the 'Hearing Voices Network' than I have in my six years of psychology training" (May, 2001).

Another participant described her first meeting as "making more sense than a lifetime of sessions with psychiatrists" (Hearing Voices Magazine, 2001/2). A psychiatric nurse (NHS) who attended a Hearing Voices meeting asked one of the speakers for treatment advice as her son had started hearing voices and she did not want him to go through the NHS psychiatric system (2005). One psychiatrist who attended a group saw his clients being discharged from the psychiatric system within one year. He found the group challenging and rewarding and it changed his perspective of his role within the care of an individual.

Coleman described the turning point in his life when a fellow voice hearer told him that his voices were real. People can find meaning in their voices and thus understand and transform them. One must try to view threatening voices as external, a third dimension. (49)

This therapy provides empowering support. It enables voice hearers to cope with their voices, increases their confidence, raises their self-esteem and reduces their isolation. This should diminish the impact or frequency of negative, persecutory voices.

Coping with Voices

A person might cope more effectively with their voices by learning to relax, taking walks, talking to others, keeping busy, holding his/her breath, making loud vocal noises, praying, isolating him/herself and receiving feedback from others. When a person is speaking or attending to other meaningful stimuli, hallucinations are less likely to occur (Slade 1974, Margo et al. 1981). Rosberg instructed a patient who constantly hallucinated to lift a chair up as high as he could for three minutes. When questioned afterwards, the patient said he did not hallucinate at all during this three minute period (2005).

Another safety valve would be to learn to control painful memories or voices by informing them that they will be addressed at a more convenient time. Ivo Wiesner, a voice hearer and spiritual healer, took his health into his own hands by searching for a positive interpretation of his experiences. He believes one has to be trained to deal with etheric sensitivities and trained to shut them off when they become overwhelming (cited in Chadwick, 1997).

The voices' presence must be acknowledged for them to be combated. A therapist would ask the client to listen to the tone of the voices, describe their physical characteristics and then concentrate on their content. The aim is not to abolish anxiety but to learn to put it in perspective. Anger can be released by punching life-size dummies or smashing cardboard boxes.

Studies

Using the approaches above, a study was conducted with twenty-one voice hearers. Seven heard fewer voices, six heard the same amount, three found the voices less disturbing/aggressive, one found that the voices had become more aggressive and four dropped out. In general, the voices were softer, kinder, more mumbled and easier to dismiss.

A ground breaking four year study of eighty children aged eight to eighteen was conducted by researchers (led by Marius Romme) at Maastricht University in Holland. The number of voice hearers halved after four years, challenging the traditional view that voices are a sign of long-term illness. 21% of the children first heard voices after suffering some sort of trauma such as sexual abuse, bereavement or illness, 37% began to hear voices after family problems such as divorce and 25% heard voices due to educational difficulties such as changing schools or bullying (Hearing Voices Magazine, 2001/2).

Romme believes voices should be rationalised and treated as real experiences rather than delusions. He interviewed hundreds of adult voice hearers in the 1990's and found that many could control their disturbing voices if they talked back to them. They were consequently less frightened of them. He hypothesised that early therapeutic intervention could prevent people from being labelled with a diagnosis and spending years in the psychiatric system. It seems that the hearing voices model should supplant the medication model. Establishing groups throughout the country would be more beneficial than building more psychiatric hospitals.

Cases

One sixteen year old boy who heard voices was admitted to a psychiatric hospital after attempting suicide. Romme and Escher began working with him and asked him to describe his voices in detail. The boy divided the voices into evil and paranormal. He subsequently greatly improved and his psychotic voices disappeared. He still heard a paranormal voice but claimed it provided moral guidance. "People can either tell their voices to go away or encourage any positive voices they hear. This can help them to control the more disturbing ones but the key is to help them understand what first triggered the voices...Voices disappear when underlying problems such as grief or bullying are resolved" (Escher, Hearing Voices Magazine, 2002).

Jenny, a paranoid 'schizophrenic', who had been abused by her step-father and sent to live with her grand-mother because her mother did not believe her, heard four voices. One was her step-father's voice who said she deserved everything, one was a protective female voice (her grand-mother), one was a female child who constantly screamed (herself as a child) and the last was a male neutral voice (her ex-husband). Firstly, Jenny had to find herself innocent. This is one of the most difficult and lonely tasks that any victim must undertake if recovery is to be a possibility. It was a painful and exhausting process, often making her voices more prominent.

Coleman, her hearing voices therapist, began to work with the voices. He firstly asked her grand-mother if she would talk to him. It took three meetings before the grand-mother stopped asking questions about why he wanted to help Jenny and why she should talk to him. These questions related to Jenny's own fears about the journey. Finally, the grand-mother agreed to help Jenny deal with the voice of the step-father. However, Jenny-the child would not engage with either Coleman or Jenny. They spent many hours attempting to forge a relationship with Jenny-the child but to no avail. Eventually they asked the grand-mother to negotiate with Jenny-the child and she slowly managed to coax her into talking. Over time, Jenny-the child stopped screaming and agreed that she had to confront the step-father. Coleman set aside two days for this to take place and Jenny was given relaxation sessions at the beginning of each day. Jenny-the child informed her step-father that it was he who should have left the house as she was innocent and he was guilty. She had the right to hate him and she was not evil. This was repeated several times, the abuser, each time, trying to regain control. However, Jenny-the child was supported by Jenny, her grand-mother and Coleman.

Afterwards the abuser's voice was still present but no longer dominant. (50) Her grand-mother's voice was now dominant but this was satisfactory as it was a positive voice. The most significant change was the voice of Jenny-the child disappearing. Jenny no longer needed to dissociate from her past. The child and adult had now integrated into Jenny-the person. Jenny has now reclaimed her life and has recovered.

Individual Programmes

Coleman and Smith have developed a recovery programme called 'Making Recovery a Reality'. They firstly assess every client and assign them to one of three groups: clients who possess the potential, motivation and desire to recover; clients who have the potential to recover but lack the confidence, desire or motivation; and clients who, for various reasons, have essentially been viewed as 'having no hope' by the system. Then a personal development plan is completed with each client. (52) In the long-term, this fast-tracks many of the more motivated clients out of the system and arranges self-help group work rather than individual sessions. The advantages of this method are: the divisions between different professions have been diluted; the approach caters for the needs of the individual (53); and the team is multi-disciplinary, often comprising nursing staff, psychology staff, occupational therapists, support workers, peer workers and medics who are all treated as necessary equals.

Another 'Home Treatment' system has been introduced by Handsworth Community Care Group with help from local voluntary groups. They provide a twenty-four hour service. The treatment is carried out in the patients' homes and 'needs-based' assessments are applied instead of medical diagnoses. Non-medical models of explanation and theory are used.

Alanen (1991), in Finland, demonstrated how effective a real community mental health system providing psychotherapy can be. Each community has a psychosis team consisting of experts in individual psychotherapy, family therapy and medication. Treatment is not decided on a national basis or even on a general local policy, nor by diagnostic category. The difficult decisions are shared by mutually respecting colleagues after interviewing the family of the client. They decide which particular combination of therapy, medication and hospitalisation would benefit the client most. Since the commencement of this system, the amount of medication used has diminished as has the necessity for hospitalisation. The data shows that it is cheaper than the previous system of community treatment where medication was administered without meaningful psychotherapy. More importantly, the clients are restored to a more human and productive life.

Hogarty et al. (1997) discovered that patients who underwent 'personal therapy' (54) were less likely to experience relapse. Also their social adjustment skills continued to improve throughout the entire three-year study.

At the end of the 18th century, Pinel and other practitioners of 'moral treatment' generated improvements for 'schizophrenics', contradicting the earlier myth of incurability. In France, England, Scotland and the USA, moral treatment produced startling results: 60-80% of patients were discharged from hospital. Its elements were simple: first, use no cruelty or humiliation, use physical force only to prevent the patient harming themselves or others but not for punishment; second, obtain as accurate a case history as possible; third, encourage work and social relations; finally, and most powerful yet seemingly unscientific, do one's best to understand the patient as an individual human being.

A specialised community setting such as a semi-permanent hostel would be beneficial. The patients may gain confidence by spending time conversing with others who have suffered similar setbacks. However, an uncharged, stable environment would be favourable at times for the patients to reflect on any improvements they have made. The patients should be encouraged to take further steps towards independence. If this goes successfully, employment could be found in a sheltered workshop. "If there had been a place like the hostel she (Susan) eventually found, where she could have the feeling of belonging to a community, both giving help and getting help...not having to hide her illness, then I do not think it would have taken nearly so long to get as far as we did and we might even have got farther" (Milner, 1969).

Case Study of Recovery

This classic case history, written in a lucid and uncomplicated style by a recovered paranoid 'schizophrenic', is more informative than any scientific theory of 'schizophrenia'.

Tracey May stated that throughout her illness, she did not know that the cause of her 'schizophrenia' was repetitive sexual abuse because all her memories had been erased. She said that 'schizophrenia' was an automatic logical response to her abuse. "If a person was to be physically violated, schizophrenia would not develop. It has to be a series of disturbing events...When an individual does not deal with situations, they build up and it might take one last incident to cause a major disturbance to the psyche. It is that simple" (May, 2002).

May proposed that, as much as patients resist, they want the therapist to reach them. (51) There is a healthy part that one can connect with behind the mask of 'schizophrenia'. Patients want to be confronted even though their rage and psychosis deny it. "I would purposely manipulate any situation to change the tables and put the spot light on those who tried to interfere in my illness. I hung onto my illness as if it was a life preserver. I was an expert in mind games. I would abuse, lie and drive anyone away who tried to break down the barriers which kept me safe. There were a few times when a couple of social workers asked me if I had been sexually abused and it triggered something deep within me. At the time, the words were not available because the illness hid the truth from my awareness but the question startled me. In a way, I did not want to run. I wanted to talk but did not know how...I replied 'no' to the question and walked away but, deep down, I wanted to stay. I think it would have been a good opportunity for the social worker to probe a little deeper."

When May did begin to recover, every incident of the abuse rushed to the surface. "I couldn't make up my mind whether to medicate myself or commit myself to a hospital. I chose neither. I wanted to feel every ounce of my pain. Inside my bedroom, I spent four weeks screaming, sobbing and doubled over in pain. I laid in a foetal position for hours. I lost a lot of weight and my body had a severe reaction whilst I let go of the pain. I actually thought I was going to have a heart attack. Flashbacks of certain events became real and terrifying. I thought I was back in the past where the sexual abuse happened...I put signs up on my walls that said things like, 'I'm OK. It won't last forever and I can survive.' I even went to a department store and bought a bat to beat my bed so that I could release my rage...I was so angry with my abusers. The pain was so great at times, I wanted to die...I even bought a rope...There were times I just wanted to shut down and not feel but it was too late. I had already opened up a way into my pain and once my eyes were opened, there was no way of stopping the process...During my recovery, there was a deep void within me because the pain was being released and there was nothing to fill the emptiness.

When the symptoms started to lose their power and disappear, I went to the bathroom and looked directly at myself in the mirror for the first time. I saw 'me'. 'I' wasn't all the terrible things that people had been saying about me for years. I was beautiful and I was a survivor. As the tears rolled down my cheeks, I knew I was going to be okay. It was just going to take time...As I walked out of the front door, I could truly hear the sound of birds and, as I looked up into the sky, I knew instantly that I was free of this horrible illness that had controlled a great many years of my life. The voices were gone. Reality was knocking at my door and I welcomed it in. I cried tears of the many losses and painful memories. I did attempt to go to therapy to talk about my experiences but I was turned down flatly because the therapist did not know how to help me. All I wanted to do was to talk about my recovery. When I asked where I could go for support, she did not know. She told me to return after I had worked everything out!"

Therapy Summary

The real tragedy of 'schizophrenia' is that Confrontation Therapy and psychoanalytic therapies work but they are not being used in wide circulation. People who have received the diagnosis of 'schizophrenia' in Britain cannot access these types of therapy on the NHS. Confrontation Therapy is an emotionally draining process for the therapist and psychoanalysis may not effect short-term benefits, like in Susan's case, so it seems they have been rendered undesirable in treating 'schizophrenia' in the UK.

Understanding the transference is essential. The more severely disturbed the patient, the more obvious the transference reactions. The severity of the symptoms in 'schizophrenia' generally means that there have been more bad things to transfer, hence the transference to the therapist will tend to be negative. Therefore the patient often does not show the therapist respect or react the way the therapist wants him/her to react. What the therapist knows does not seem to work. Thus the therapist often feels scared. It is not an accident that the most illuminating discussions of negative countertransference have emerged from therapists who have worked with 'schizophrenics' (eg. Searles, 1965). The 'schizophrenic' has intense feelings of fear and terror but they are masked and denied. Sometimes the therapist may, all too successfully, empathise with this terror and withdraw from the patient instead of admitting that he is feeling the patient's terror and showing that he can bear it.

Analysts must make an active verbal effort to establish a relationship with their patients. It is not the analyst's job to decide whether events remembered are factually true but to work with the patient's constantly changing psychic reality. "I believe that for certain patients, a psychoanalytically oriented, investigative psychotherapy, with the goal of increased self-understanding and personal growth, can be successful even in the face of vulnerability to psychotic disorganisation" (Levy, 1993).

Therapists must listen without judgement and confront in a supportive way. They must have the courage to persist with patients who verbally reject them and the wisdom and skill to tease out the logic of irrational speech. In chronic cases, elements of the Confrontation approach should be employed to combat the patient's entrenched, dysfunctional behaviour.

The patient must learn adult forms of communication and achieve insight into the role that the past has played in current problems. Fromm-Reichman was calm, optimistic and sensitive to the unconscious meaning of behaviour. She attributed her patients' aloofness to a wish to avoid the rebuffs suffered in childhood. In helping a person to become explicitly aware of the events that have influenced their life, the persistent effects of these events on their future can be mitigated and indeed radically modified. "Understanding origins can sometimes lead to cures" (Slater, 1996).

Auditory hallucinations could be tackled by a Hearing Voices therapist. Self-understanding must be emphasised and psychotic manifestations should be regarded as reflections of intra-psychic conflict and repetitions of past experience. Goethe said that to understand people, we must consider process over time, rather than thinking about a particular moment. "The present is often viewed so determinedly in terms of past experience that it takes a lot of careful work before the present can be seen for itself – as separate and different from the past" (Casement, 1990).

There is a considerable body of evidence to suggest that therapists providing high levels of accurate empathy, non-possessive warmth and genuineness have positive effects on 'schizophrenic' patients (Truax, 1970). The most effective therapists are possibly those who have previously suffered yet can maintain a detached, objective attitude. Allen believes that there are five stages in human development: Innocence; Victimhood; Victorhood; Teacher and Master. The best support network would consist of recovered 'schizophrenics' helping those still suffering. A Chinese proverb states, "To know the road ahead, ask those who are coming back."

One of the main weaknesses of psychiatrists is that they rely on previous notes made about the patient rather than starting without pre-conceived ideas. Thus nothing can change for the patient. "We must search our hearts, be ready to be stripped of any comfort in believing... Faith must know that it can never know, and must be aware of the guile of its own need to believe" (Casement, 1990).

Psychiatrists present the patient with no or little hope of recovery. Hope is essential as it fights fear and nurtures courage. Receiving respect and warmth breaks through the isolation and helps one to feel worthy and alive. Anger can sustain the patient's stubborn refusal to accept the psychiatrist's dire predictions and can protect his/her hopes and dreams.

Therapists must be aware that there can be a great risk of suicide when a patient is nearing the final stages of the therapeutic process. "What a dangerous moment it can be when someone recovering from a long mental illness suddenly realises what has been the cost of the illness. I knew how the danger of suicide can be increased at such times" (Milner, 1969).

Concluding Remarks

The negative symptoms of 'schizophrenia' are found in acute depression and also may be consequences of neuroleptic medication (see Chapter 3). In Chapter 3, it was also suggested that the only symptoms of 'schizophrenia' that are not consequences of medication and institutionalisation are hallucinations, delusions, catatonic behaviour and thought disorder. Hallucinations and thought disorder are symptoms of PTSD (see Chapter 4), catatonic behaviour is a result of suffering trauma and delusions derive from real events in a person's past. Thus it seems that the disorder of 'schizophrenia' is neither valid nor reliable.

When attempting, with success, to have her diagnosis withdrawn, Janet Frame was interviewed many times and had several tests which proved her brainwaves were "more normal than normal" (Frame, 1982/4/5). After a long meeting with a team of doctors, Sir Aubrey declared that she had never suffered from 'schizophrenia' and should never have been admitted to a mental hospital. She had longed to be rid of the label but was also unwilling to part with it for fear of the unknown. "Schizophrenia had been an accomplishment removing ordinary responsibility from the sufferer...Now, I had only my ordinary self to use to try and explain my distress" (ibid.). In other words, being given a diagnosis prevents one from searching for the reasons behind one's unhappiness or odd behaviour.

Chronic conditions of fear, tension, horror, disgust and grief are the pre-requisites for 'schizophrenia'. The severity of the illness will depend on both the trauma and the interpretation of it. (55) The differences in vulnerability can be accounted for by the quantity and quality of the stress. Given enough stress, I believe every person has the potential to develop 'schizophrenic' symptoms. However, the intensity of the stress is usually determined by its conscious and unconscious meanings. Here, psychoanalysis is necessary as it is the only type of therapy which has the capacity to delve into the unconscious to uncover these meanings. Patients must make contact with the 'other' in themselves.

Coleman believes that psychosis is a response to feelings of loneliness and alienation. He believes his own voices appeared to alert him to the fact that his life was not whole. "Because of my continual refusal to acknowledge the past, my inner self was left with no option but to externalise my experiences through the introduction of the voices" (Coleman, 1999).

The culmination of unexpressed, unresolved traumas could cause ego-splitting and dissociation (see Chapter 4). The fragile ego of the 'schizophrenic' is unable to handle extreme stress and so splits or regresses. Malign splittings of the ego are defences against unbearable feelings.

When one has to endure trauma after trauma, one attempts to escape from these intolerable conditions. Withdrawal is usually an attempt to create a reality that is preferable to reality in the external world. (56) A compromise is negotiated by the psyche between the instinct of self-preservation and the prohibitions against deception or flight which were rendered impossible. 'The desired state of numbness' is often referred to by sufferers (Sassoon). This becomes an important psychological resource.

These are terrified human beings whose great fear leads to a disintegration and dissolution of their identity. They may harbour annihilation fantasies and fear destruction. They retreat until they are surrounded by defences. The fear is processed by the person into a number of symptoms such as hallucinations, delusions and paranoia. These defences are chosen to protect the person and are based on the totality of his/her prior experience. They may appear inefficient, illogical, irrational and extremely confusing to an outsider and even to the patient. These chosen defences and symptoms may reduce the fear but a new identity emerges with its own logic and language that is termed 'schizophrenia'. This system of life acts as a survival mechanism that becomes resistant to change. "Madness is a desperate attempt to preserve the self" (Coleman, 1999).

'Schizophrenics' are constantly attempting to solve their problems but they deal with symbols because confronting the real problems is too frightening. Only when the symbolic act, or symptom, and the original traumatic experience are re-connected in consciousness can the person begin to recover. Medication cannot break down the defences built, nor can it interpret these symbols. It can only provide symptom relief for as long as it is used. Confrontation Therapy can break down defences. Once a relationship has been formed and changes have been made, the patient will gain insights into their condition thus enabling psychosocial rehabilitation and psychoanalytic psychotherapy to be employed successfully. Psychoanalytic psychotherapy is invaluable in interpreting symbols. Interpretations will synthesise the split in the self and make it possible for anxiety to be experienced gradually. However, analysts must guard against making too many interpretations as this can remove responsibility from the patient (see 'Susan' in Chapter 5).

"If the patient, the therapist and the setting can tolerate it, the psychotherapy is best conducted without medication. If the patient asks for it, or the therapist is uncomfortable talking with disorganised patients or the setting requires it, medication can be used, but it should be withdrawn as rapidly as the patient can tolerate. Medication as an adjunct makes behavioural control easier to attain, but slows down the rate of underlying change.

This is because medications damp affective responses which are helpful to the patient. But affective responses during the therapy session are also a part of the process of change"(Karon, 2001).

In order for treatment to reach its maximum effectiveness, a series of treatment modalities must act in a compatible manner with each other. Every form of treatment has limitations. Each independent effort alone is not enough. The different disciplines must collaborate harmoniously with one another. The most effective treatment often requires the sophisticated integration of several pharmacological, psychosocial and rehabilitative strategies. While medications can ameliorate some symptoms and rehabilitation can improve social and vocational skills, a psychotherapeutic relationship can address the human aspects of suffering from a serious and long-term disorder and trace the origins of symptoms.

"As psychiatrists, we are first and foremost physicians" (Enoch, 1990). Psychologists have been content to accept that they work with neurotics and psychiatrists work with psychotics. In the late 1980's and early 1990's, some medical practitioners blocked psychologists from obtaining hospital privileges. However, psychological theories are necessary to account for the complexities of mind and interaction, including both pathogenesis and treatment of mental disorders. Interdisciplinary squabbles are nothing new but they seldom contribute to advancements in knowledge or improvements in patient care. Each profession must respect its limits and the autonomy of its neighbour and avoid assertions that penetrate and belittle the other's domain. Each must be compatible, consistent and congruent with one another at their boundary. "Growth occurs at the place where differences meet, confront each other and interpenetrate" (Milner, 1969).

The psychiatrist views the 'schizophrenic' as biologically sick and the therapist views the 'schizophrenic' as well-defended by psychotic behaviour. Neurobiology is necessary to account for mental phenomena and 'higher order' theoretical domains.

Pavlov (1973) wrote, "How could we separate from one another what the physiologist calls the temporal connection and what the psychologist calls association? In this case, the one is completely merged, completely absorbed by and identified with the other" (cited in Bentall, 1990).

If, in a hypothetical future, society was scientifically sophisticated but illiterate, how would the semantic content or story-line be assessed when reading a book? Physical or chemical examinations would correctly identify it as a book but a book cannot be reducible to the mere motion of molecules (Rose, 1984). A person cannot be reducible to a random collection of symptoms.

It is not denied that biological factors are of relevance but they are often severely over-emphasised thus commanding more attention than the damaging emotional effects of environmental conditions such as abuse, violence, low self-esteem, degrading life experiences, poverty, unemployment, low social status, social estrangement, powerlessness, loneliness, social isolation and social marginality. We make the world and its people what they are. It is rarely the case that a genetic endowment is totally and utterly inevitable in its effects.

"Psychoanalysis has talked a lot about the accidental factors in aetiology and little about the constitutional ones...we assume that the two sets regularly act jointly in bringing about the observed result. Endowment and Chance determine a man's fate - rarely or never one of these powers alone. The amount of aetiological effectiveness to be attributed to each of them can only be arrived at in every individual case separately" (Freud, 1912, cited in Schachter, 1993).

Services and treatments should be tailored to each individual. Recent policy changes favouring 'care in the community' reflect a movement that has long been developing (Murphy, 1991). There should be provision for twenty-four hour crisis help. Close collaboration between professionals of different disciplines and agencies would provide the most effective treatment. This would be expensive but might not exceed the cost of supplying three-hundred thousand patients with a life-time supply of neuroleptic medication or funding further fruitless biological studies of 'schizophrenia'.

Further research should target areas that provide answers to questions such as:
'Why can some 'schizophrenics' recover and others not?'

'Why do similar traumas produce different reactions in different people?'

'Why do hallucinations appear real to psychotics yet unreal to 'normal' people?'

'Are there changes in the brain when hallucinations occur?'

'If the brain changes in the face of trauma, can it ever change back?' Rose et al. (1984) proposed that "Just as drugs change behaviour, so will altered behaviour imposed by talking therapies change brains" (cited in Bentall, 1990).

'When, if ever, do organic pathological changes become so extensive that they are irreversible?'

"Too often, the complexities in the 'schizophrenic' process are blamed for the lack of significant progress with the seriously mentally ill patient. However, it is in my considered professional opinion, as a result of forty-three years of experience, that the fault lies with the professionals rather than with the patient and his/her condition. If we do not try or give it the effort it requires, progress doesn't take place" (Rosberg, 1999).

Better education for psychiatrists and the general public about mental disorders and the democratisation of mental health services would be a good starting point. (57) A simple classroom situation where both patients and psychiatrists learn about hallucinations would 'normalise' this symptom and reduce the stigma attached to 'schizophrenia'. Universities must include the teaching of the Direct Confrontation method and Psychosocial Rehabilitation in their curriculum. Thomas Malone (cited in Rosberg, 1999) discovered that good psychological treatment can be taught successfully to experienced and inexperienced therapists if they are able to relax their prior beliefs about psychotherapy. These students can then express themselves with more intuition and spontaneity. William Anthony PhD (Boston University), a distinguished contributor in social rehabilitation, said, "Psychology as a field has not focused its training in the area of serious mental illness" (cited in Rosberg, 1999).

Rufus May recovered from 'schizophrenia' and no longer needs medication. He trained for ten years to be a psychologist but never disclosed his diagnosis as this would have rendered him 'ill-qualified' for the course. He questioned himself, "What if I managed to infiltrate the mental health system and change things from within?" Unfortunately, this is perhaps the only way the psychiatric system can be challenged.

Recovery is not a gift from doctors but the responsibility of all individuals. It requires self-confidence, self-esteem, self-awareness and self-acceptance. The system may create the diagnosis but the patient often reinforces it. Recovery can only be achieved when the paradigm is shifted from one of biological reductionism to one of societal and personal development. Too often, psychiatrists perceive recovery to be 'maintaining the patient in a stable condition', regardless of issues such as adverse effects of medication or even the expressed wish of the client (Coleman, 1999). They concentrate on preventing relapse rather than the possibility of cure. This results in a defensive practice method. "In order for the journey of recovery to be successful, it is important to deconstruct the power of the psychiatric system and reconstruct power as a personal commodity" (Coleman, 1999).

Bibliography

American Psychiatric Association (1994) *Diagnostic and Statistical Manual of Mental Disorders - Fourth Edition (DSM-IV)*. Washington DC.

Bannister, D. (1968) *The Logical Requirements of Research into Schizophrenia*. The British Journal of Psychiatry. Volume 114, p.181-188.

Bassman, R. (2001) *Overcoming the Impossible: My Journey through Schizophrenia*. "Psychology Today". Internet.

Bentall, R.P. (1990) *Reconstructing Schizophrenia*. London: Routledge.

Bentall, R.P., Jackson, H.F. and Pilgrim, D. (1988) *Abandoning the Concept of Schizophrenia: Some Implications of Validity Arguments for Psychological Research into Psychotic Phenomena*. The British Journal of Clinical Psychology. Volume 27, p.303-324.

Bhugra, D. and Bahl, V. (1999) *Ethnicity: An Agenda for Mental Health*. London: Gaskell, Royal College of Psychiatrists.

Bion, W.R. (1957) *Differentiation of the Psychotic from the Non-*

Psychotic Personalities. The International Journal of Psychoanalysis. Volume 38, p.266-275.

Bion W.R. (1980) *Bion in New York and Sao Paulo.* Perthshire: Clunie Press.

Breier, A. and Strauss, J.S. (1983) *Self-Control in Psychiatric Disorders.* The Archives of General Psychiatry. Volume 40, p.1141-1145.

Carpenter, W.T., McGlashan, T.H. and Strauss, J.S. (1977) *The Treatment of Acute Schizophrenia Without Drugs - An Investigation of some Current Assumptions.* The American Journal of Psychiatry. Volume 134, p.14-20.

Casement, P. (1985) *On Learning from the Patient.* London: Routledge.

Casement, P. (1990) *Further Learning from the Patient.* Brunner-Routledge.

Chadwick, P.K. (1997) *Schizophrenia - The Positive Perspective.* London: Routledge.

Coleman, R. (1999) *Recovery: an Alien Concept?* Gloucester: Handsell Publishing.

Davison, G.C. and Neale, J.M. (1994, first pub. 1974) *Abnormal Psychology.* John Wiley and Sons, Inc. Sixth edition.

Escher (2000/1) *Hearing Voices* Magazine (2001 and 2002). Manchester: Hearing Voices Network.

Etherington, K. (2000) *Narrative Approaches to Working with Adult Male Survivors of Child Sexual Abuse - The Clients', the Counsellor's and the Researcher's Story.* London: Jessica Kingsley Publishers Ltd.

Frame, J. (1984) *An Angel at my Table. Autobiography 2.* Flamingo, an imprint of Harper Collins Publishers.

Frame, J. (1991, first pub. 1982/4/5) *An Autobiography.* G. Braziller Inc.

Freud, S. (1911) *Psychoanalytic Notes upon an Autobiographical Account of a Case of Paranoia.* Case Histories II. (1990) Translated and edited by J. Strachey. London: Penguin Books Ltd.

Frude, N. (1998) *Understanding Abnormal Psychology.* Oxford: Blackwell Publishers.

Hearing Voices Magazine (2001 and 2002). Manchester: Hearing Voices Network.

Karon, B.P. (2001) *The Tragedy of Schizophrenia without Psychotherapy.* The Frieda Fromm-Reichmann Lecture. The Michigan Psychoanalytic Council.

Klein, M. (1946) *Notes on Some Schizoid Mechanisms.* "The Selected Melanie Klein". (1991, first pub. 1986) Edited by J. Mitchell. London: Penguin Books Ltd.

Lacan, J. (1955/6) *The Psychoses - The Seminar of Jacques Lacan.* Edited by J-A. Miller. Book III. (1993) Translated by R. Grigg. London: Routledge.

Laing, R.D. (1965, first pub. 1959) *The Divided Self.* Middlesex: Penguin Books Ltd.

Laing, R.D. and Esterson, A. (1970, first pub. 1964) *Sanity, Madness and the Family.* Middlesex: Penguin Books Ltd.

Levy, S.T. (1993) *Countertransference Aspects in the Treatment of Schizophrenia.* "Psychotherapy and Medication - A Dynamic Integration". Edited by M. Schachter. New Jersey: Jason Aronson Inc.

May, R. (6/2/2001) *Taking a Stand.* Broadcast on Radio 4, presented by F. Keane, produced by J. Beresford.

May, T. (2002) *Recovery is Possible.* Internet: www.schizophrenia-help.com/tracey.htm

McGrath, J. (2001) BioSpace News: Schizophrenia. Internet.

Mednick, S.A., Schulsinger, F., Higgens, J. and Bell, B. (1974, first pub. 1968) *Genetics, Environment and Psychopathology.* North-Holland Publishing Company.

Milner, M. (1969) *The Hands of the Living God - An Account of Psychoanalytic Treatment.* London: The Hogarth Press Ltd.

Moate, M. and Enoch, D. (1992, first pub. 1990) *Schizophrenia: Voices in the Dark.* Eastbourne: Kingsway Publications Ltd.

Nasar, S. (1998) *A Beautiful Mind.* Faber and Faber Limited.

Nevins, D.B. (1993) *Adverse Response to Neuroleptics in Schizophrenia.* "Psychotherapy and Medication - A Dynamic Integration". Edited by M. Schachter. New Jersey: Jason Aronson Inc.

Robbins, M. (1992) *Psychoanalytic and Biological Approaches to Mental Illness: Schizophrenia.* The Journal of the American Psychoanalytic Association. Volume 40, p.425-454.

Rodríguez, L.S. (1999) *Psychoanalysis with Children - History, Theory and Practice.* London: Free Association Books Ltd.

Rosenfeld, H. (1952) *Transference-Phenomena and Transference Analysis in an Acute Catatonic Schizophrenic Patient.* British Journal of Psychoanalysis, Volume 33, p. 457-463.

Rosberg, J. (1999) *Newsletter of the Schizophrenia Help Home Page.* Internet: www.schizophrenia-help.com/feb99.htm

Schachter, M. (1993) *Psychotherapy and Medication - A Dynamic Integration.* Jason Aronson Inc.

Schreber, D.P. (1902/1955) *Memoirs of my Nervous Illness.* Translated and edited by I. Macalpine and R. Hunter. Harvard University Press.

Scott, M.J. and Palmer, S. (2000) *Trauma and Post-Traumatic Stress Disorder.* London: Cassell.

Searles, H.F. (1993, first pub. 1965) *Collected Papers on Schizophrenia and Related Subjects.* Karnac Books.

Slater, L. (1997, first pub. 1996) *Welcome to my Country - A Therapist's Memoir of Madness.* London: Penguin Books Ltd.

Soler, C. (publication date unavailable) *A Passion in Transference.* The Newsletter of the Freudian Field. Edited by E. Ragland-Sullivan.

Stevens, J.R. (1982) *Neuropathology of Schizophrenia.* The Archives of General Psychiatry. Volume 39, p.1131-1139.

Survivors Swindon (2001/2) Internet.

Szasz, T.S. (1972, first pub. 1962) *The Myth of Mental Illness.* London: Granada Publishing Ltd., Paladin.

Szasz, T.S. (1979) *Schizophrenia: The Sacred Symbol of Psychiatry.* Oxford University Press.

Truax, C.B. (1970) *Effects of Client-Centred Psychotherapy with Schizophrenic Patients: Nine years Pre-therapy and Nine Years Post-therapy Hospitalisation.* Consulting and Clinical Psychology, Volume 35, p.417-422.

de Valdo (2000/1) *Hearing Voices* Magazine (2001 and 2002). Manchester: Hearing Voices Network.

de Waelhens, A. (1984) *Phenomenology and Psychoanalysis: Reflections in Reference to the book of A. de Waelhens, Schizophrenia.* The Journal of Phenomenological Psychology. Volume 15, Part 1, p.1-19.

Willick, M.S. (1993) *The Deficit Syndrome in Schizophrenia: Psychoanalytic and Neurobiological Perspectives.* The Journal of the American Psychoanalytic Association. Volume 41, Part 4, p.1135-1157.

Winnicott, D.W. (1958) *Collected Papers: Through Paediatrics to Psycho-Analysis.* London: Tavistock Publications.

Endnotes

1 'Dissociation' is a disconnection between mental processes, such as thoughts, feelings, meanings and sometimes one's sense of identity.
2 The Diagnostic and Statistical Manual of Mental Disorders.
3 At least one person a week dies as a result of neuroleptic medication (National MIND figures).
4 'Transference' is where the original source of conflict is displaced onto the analyst.
5 There is no court of appeal when the diagnosis is made yet it is clearly elusive.
6 Positive symptoms reflect a distortion of normal functions.
7 This is a side effect of neuroleptic medication.
8 inability to gauge whether a stimulus is self-generated or perceived.
9 Her patients informed her of this after emerging from the stupor.
10 For 'schizophrenics', "much of what seems sexual has to do with orality: that is, infantile feelings, survival and the early mother-child relationship" (Karon, 2001).
11 Negative symptoms reflect a diminution or loss of normal functions.
12 These could be caused by sexual abuse. One attempts to render oneself unattractive to the opposite sex (see Chapter 4).
13 The total genetic make-up of an individual, consisting of inherited genes, is referred to as the 'genotype'. This genotype is the unobservable, physiological genetic

constitution. However, the totality of observable characteristics is referred to as the 'phenotype'. The genotype is fixed at birth whereas the phenotype alters and is generally viewed as the product of an interaction between the genotype and experience. Therefore it is incorrect to speak of the direct inheritance of 'schizophrenia'. Only the genotypes for this disorder can be inherited. A predisposition (diathesis) may be inherited but not the disorder itself. "Stress is required to render this predisposition an observable pathology" (Davison and Neale, 1994).

14 for examples, see Laing (1964).

15 Neuroleptics produce narcissistic changes which are defensive in nature and cause depersonalisation. There is conflict in the ego and there are attempts to solve these conflicting identifications and self images. The state of depersonalisation in 'schizophrenics' is a defence of the ego which attempts to recover and maintain its intactness by opposing, detaching and disowning the regressed, diseased part.

16 The DSM-IV admits that "neuroleptic medications often produce extrapyramidal side effects that closely resemble affective flattening or avolition" (DSM-IV, 1994).

17 The diagnosis of 'schizophrenia' is warranted if prominent delusions or hallucinations are present for at least a month. This is an arbitrary length of time and shows a severe lack of understanding. Once a person begins to hear audible voices, they can remain for life. Explanations of the aetiology of hallucinations and delusions follow (see Chapter 4).

18 Thought disorder is a symptom of 'depression', 'mania', 'aphasia' (see 'Reliability' above) and PTSD (see Chapter 4).

19 Metaphor illuminates childhood scenes that one cannot translate into words and communicates understanding on many levels.

20 as survivors of rape often describe (see Joan's description below).

21 This does not mean that 54% did not suffer from an

independent life event. Perhaps some did but concealed it due to repression or they could have suffered over a long period of time.

22 "I don't think they (flashbacks) will ever go completely but they are fading and are easier to cope with" (Survivor of the Purley train crash, cited in Scott and Palmer, 2000).

23 Abnormalities of this area of the brain have also been identified with 'schizophrenia', signifying that traumatic memories are a feature of this disorder.

24 as in Susan's drawings (see Chapter 5).

25 as Milner did in the Susan case (see Chapter 5).

26 'If I'm already dead, I cannot be killed.' If a person is already in pieces, they cannot be broken.

27 Joan was able to provide a clear statement of the phenomenology of her psychosis in straightforward, simple language. She only felt real because of the reactions she could produce in her loving therapist, Laing.

28 This seems to favour the 'Confrontation' approach (see Chapter 6).

29 There are a series of careful empirical studies demonstrating an unconscious defence, termed 'Pathogenesis', measurable from the TAT, to be more prevalent in parents of 'schizophrenics' (Karon and Widener, 1994). This relates to whether one does or does not take into account the conflicting needs of a dependent when his/her needs differ from one's own.

30 Freud (1924) defines a weak ego as one that cannot adapt to reality so repudiates it and regresses.

31 apart from Pao (1979), Giovacchini (1986) and Robbins (1992).

32 when Milner no longer needed a cigarette.

33 Defence mechanisms always hinder recovery.

34 She wrote "O Moon of my Delight" to Susan (Milner, 1969).

35 Perhaps Susan's mother walked out to save her children from her murderous impulses towards them. In the analysis, Susan expressed a fear of taking the dangerous mother within herself.

36 Susan could not understand duality of meaning, perhaps

due to the fact that she could not recognise that she was separate from her mother.

37 Perhaps 'Confrontation therapy' (see Chapter 6) would have disrupted this identification.

38 This was portrayed in her drawings.

39 Water, like air, stands for an environment that both accepts and permits a feeling of the flowing together of the self and the world.

40 Certain kinds of mastery defeat themselves by destroying what is to be mastered.

41 The lack of opportunity for and recognition of reparative activities can greatly encourage psychotic states of mind (Milner, 1969).

42 Milner recognised that, when accepted, the 'schizophrenic's urge to be nothing could become part of the process that leads to a new birth, both of self and other.

43 the opposite mechanism to projection.

44 a sadistic attack and triumph over Rosenfeld.

45 Frequently, however, the 'schizophrenic's lack of interest and withdrawal is attributed solely to his auto-erotism.

46 Nunberg also noticed how his patient sometimes felt confused with him. He talked as if Nunberg and himself were the same person. Nunberg suggested that a narcissistic identification had taken place. It is the desire for the object which led to the disappearance of distance between the ego and object. Thus the patient had taken possession of the object and had incorporated it into the ego.

47 This would be unnecessary if all therapists and psychiatrists were genuinely caring and competent.

48 'Countertransference' is where the psychotherapist transfers his own feelings onto the patient.

49 Freud recognised that an external threat is easier to deal with than an internal one in the 'Rat Man' case (1911).

50 The abuse could not be undone.

51 This echoes Joan's views (see Chapter 4) and the 'Confrontation' approach to therapy (see Chapter 6).

52 see copy in Appendix, designed by the Assertive Outreach

Team in the Sutton and Kingstanding Locality, North Birmingham.

53 Coleman adopts the 'PIE' model - 'Play It by Ear'. The service is created around the person rather than fitting the person into existing services.

54 'Personal therapy' is a three-part process specifically tailored to the needs of the individual patient. In the months after discharge, the therapist develops a rapport with the patient and conducts some basic psychological education. Then the patient learns a variety of ways to deal with stress, including social skills and relaxation exercises. Finally, the patient tries to understand their poor social behaviour, other peoples' reactions and their symptoms.

55 Target (1999) explained that procedural memory, built up from earliest infancy, carries knowledge about what to expect from the world and how to deal with it. This knowledge is demonstrated in behaviour rather than being communicated verbally. Psychoanalysis offers a unique way to understand and treat responses that are based on procedural memories of trauma.

56 Laing practised mental withdrawal to escape his feelings of terror and rage when he was beaten by his father.

57 When Susan became an assistant nurse in a ward of a mental hospital, she was given no instructions of how to deal with the patients, some of whom were violent.

APPENDIX

ASSERTIVE OUTREACH TEAM

SUTTON AND KINGSTANDING LOCALITY - PERSONAL RECOVERY PLAN

WHAT IS THE PURPOSE OF THIS PLAN?

This recovery plan is intended to help you identify what you need to make your life how you would like it to be.

> It can help you (and the people who support you) to look positively at your strengths, needs, hopes, wishes, difficulties and experiences and make sense of these things in order to move forward.

It may help professionals to base their services upon what YOU REALLY WANT and not what THEY THINK YOU NEED. It may help them to identify their own training needs and plan appropriately for the future of mental health services.

WHO HAS DEVELOPED THIS PLAN?

This plan has been developed by people who have used the mental health system. Staff members have also contributed. We realised that professional 'assessments' frequently concentrate too much upon difficulties, diagnoses and symptoms and neglect strengths, priorities and positives. We believe that it would be more beneficial to concentrate on strengths, as strengths can be developed to overcome some difficulties.

People who have used similar plans have commented that writing things down helped them to make sense of their experiences and focus upon what is really important. They can then consider new ways of moving forward and develop their confidence.

WHAT DO I NEED TO DO TO USE THIS PLAN?

You do not have to complete this recovery plan if you do not want to. If you do choose to use this plan, you can decide:

when to complete it (for example, it may be difficult to complete it when you are feeling distressed).

how long to take (there is no time limit. You can work through the plan at your own pace).

who you want to help you complete it (another person may help you to make sense of certain questions. This person could be someone who knows you well).

where it should be kept (you may want to keep the finished plan at home or you could ask your key-worker to lock it somewhere safe).

who can see it (what is written in this plan belongs to you, so only you can decide who sees it).

You can leave questions out if they do not apply to you and you can go back and change things. You have probably been 'assessed' before by professional staff. This is different – YOU are in control of this and you can use it to request specific support.

There are some things you MUST do if you decide to complete this plan. If you cannot do the following three things then you are not ready to use the plan:

1 BE HONEST WITH YOURSELF
2 TAKE RESPONSIBILITY FOR YOURSELF
3 BE COMMITTED TO YOUR OWN RECOVERY

WHAT DOES RECOVERY MEAN?

Recovery means different things to different people. It is not necessarily about the complete disappearance of mental distress and symptoms. For some of us, it means learning to cope with our difficulties, gaining control of our lives, achieving our goals, developing our skills and fulfilling our dreams.

Nothing can happen without a considerable amount of effort from you. It will not happen overnight. There are seven stages to this plan. You may choose to fill them in one stage at a time.

STAGE ONE

WHAT RECOVERY MEANS TO ME: (use this space to write what you think recovery is)

STAGE TWO - *ABOUT MYSELF*

MY NAME IS:

THE PLACE I WAS BORN IS:

SOME THINGS I REMEMBER ABOUT MY CHILDHOOD ARE:

AT SCHOOL I:

SOME THINGS I REMEMBER ABOUT MY ADOLESCENCE ARE:

IMPORTANT EVENTS IN MY ADULT LIFE HAVE BEEN:

THINGS I CURRENTLY DO IN A TYPICAL DAY ARE:

MY HOBBIES AND INTERESTS ARE:

PLACES I LIKE GOING ARE:

I RELAX BY:

RELATIONSHIPS WITH MY FAMILY ARE:

RELATIONSHIPS WITH MY FRIENDS ARE:

THINGS I LIKE ABOUT MYSELF AND MY STRENGTHS ARE:

THINGS OTHER PEOPLE LIKE ABOUT ME ARE:

THINGS I DO WHICH OTHER PEOPLE FIND DIFFICULT ARE: (you may wish to mention harming yourself, talking to voices, etc.)

I EXPRESS MY FEELINGS BY:

MY MOST IMPORTANT ACHIEVEMENTS HAVE BEEN:

MY POSSESSIONS INCLUDE:

MY MONEY SITUATION IS:

MY PHYSICAL HEALTH IS:

THINGS I CONSIDER SPIRITUALLY AND CULTURALLY IMPORTANT INCLUDE:

THINGS I CONSIDER IMPORTANT ABOUT MY SEXUALITY INCLUDE:

THINGS I VALUE IN LIFE ARE:

ANYTHING ELSE THAT I HAVE NOT ALREADY WRITTEN:

STAGE THREE - *DIFFICULTIES*

THINGS I FIND DIFFICULT IN MY LIFE ARE:

I WOULD DESCRIBE MY MENTAL HEALTH AS: (you might mention your experiences, thoughts and emotions)

CAN YOU RELATE ANY STRESSFUL SITUATIONS YOU HAVE EXPERIENCED TO YOUR MENTAL HEALTH DIFFICULTIES?

HOW HAVE YOUR DIFFICULTIES AFFECTED YOUR QUALITY OF LIFE? (this list may help you to answer this question: self esteem, confidence, concentration, relationships with others, socialising, personal care: e.g. hygiene, safety, etc., domestic skills: e.g. cooking or cleaning, physical health and fitness, finances or accommodation, work or study, leisure or hobbies, other peoples' attitudes and behaviour towards you, your goals for the future)

STAGE FOUR - *COPING*

HOW DO YOU COPE WITH YOUR DIFFICULTIES/ILLNESS? (the following list may be helpful: talking to other people about your difficulties and feelings, writing things down in a diary, reading information about your experiences, shouting at people, trying to think of solutions to problems, writing down small steps towards a solution, asking other people to help you, crying, positive thinking, relaxation tapes, doing something to take your mind off things, pretending things are not happening, drinking or taking drugs, hiding in bed and worrying, blaming other people, praying, using alternative therapies: e.g. aromatherapy, taking medication, self harm)

WHAT DOES NOT HELP YOU COPE?

WHO HELPS YOU AND HOW DO THEY HELP? (you might mention friends, fellow service users, family, partner, doctors, CPNs, OTs, social workers, etc.)

STAGE FIVE - *THE MENTAL HEALTH SYSTEM AND TREATMENTS*

DESCRIBE THE TREATMENTS YOU HAVE HAD FROM MENTAL HEALTH SERVICES. HAVE THEY HELPED YOU? IF SO, HOW? (refer to the following list to help you: medication, ECT, counselling, psychotherapy, physiotherapy, behavioural therapy, support with social activities, support with practical skills, support in finding work or education activities, stress or anxiety management, anger management)

WERE YOU GIVEN A CHOICE REGARDING THE TREATMENTS YOU WERE OFFERED?

WERE YOU HAPPY WITH THE ENVIRONMENT IN WHICH YOU WERE GIVEN ANY OF THESE TREATMENTS?

ARE THERE ANY TREATMENTS YOU HAVE NOT BEEN OFFERED THAT YOU BELIEVE WOULD HELP YOU?

IF YOU HAVE BEEN AN IN-PATIENT, WHAT WAS THE EXPERIENCE LIKE?

DESCRIBE THE ATTITUDE OF MENTAL HEALTH STAFF TOWARDS YOU.

HAVE YOU BEEN GIVEN A DIAGNOSIS?

WHAT IS YOUR ATTITUDE TOWARDS THIS DIAGNOSIS?

DESCRIBE ANY SIDE EFFECTS FROM YOUR MEDICATION.

WOULD YOU LIKE TO MEET WITH OTHERS WHO HAVE EXPERIENCED OR ARE EXPERIENCING SIMILAR DIFFICULTIES FOR MUTUAL SUPPORT?

STAGE SIX - *PLANS FOR CHANGE*

WRITE DOWN THE THINGS YOU WOULD LIKE TO DO IN THE FUTURE (you might include relationships, hobbies, work, housing, education, leisure, etc.)

STAGE SEVEN - *YOUR PERSONAL DEVELOPMENT PLAN*

This stage involves looking back through everything you have written and deciding on the most important things you need to change in order to work towards your recovery. It will probably help you to work on this stage with someone who knows you well as this can be the most difficult part to complete. Include difficulties you want to overcome but also the positive things you want to develop.

THINGS ABOUT MY LIFE I WOULD LIKE TO CHANGE ARE:

WHAT SHOULD BE THE OUTCOME OF THIS CHANGE?

STEPS I NEED TO TAKE TO MAKE THE CHANGE ARE:

PEOPLE I WOULD LIKE TO HELP ME ARE:

BARRIERS TO ACHIEVING THIS CHANGE ARE:

Repeat this process for each change that you wish to make. Remember to review your progress and record how much you have achieved in fulfilling your goals.

Printed in the United Kingdom
by Lightning Source UK Ltd.
113936UKS00001B/82-105